THE PIONEERS
GLOUCESTER CITY ASSOCIATION FOOTBALL CLUB
1883-1914
LEAGUE FOOTBALL STATISTICS
By Timothy RD Clark

A BOOKLET TO CELEBRATE THE
125TH ANNIVERSARY
OF THE FORMATION OF A
GLOUCESTER ASSOCIATION FOOTBALL CLUB
Profits go to the
Gloucester City Supporters Trust

ISBN 978-0-9557425-0-7

Published by TigerTimbo Publications,
2 Rosemary Close,
Abbeydale,
Gloucester GL4 5TL

© Timothy RD Clark 2007

First published December 2007

All rights reserved. No part of this publication may be reproduced or copied in any manner without the prior permission in writing of the author.

Dedicated to Sydney Walter Clark
1912-2004
"From mud, through blood, to the green fields beyond."

FOREWORD

I have only known Tim Clark well for the past couple of seasons, but I commend him and this labour of love, *The Pioneers*, most warmly to you.

Extraordinarily, though Tim and I stood on the Gloucester City terraces at both Longlevens and Horton Road in bygone times, I suppose that we were absorbed by the action on the pitch and so never noticed each other. At Meadow Park, and latterly at The New Lawn, Forest Green, however, we have both taken to sitting in the stand and not far from each other, so that we have come to chat regularly.

We are both enthusiasts for Gloucester City but perhaps Tim has more to show for it than I do, on account of his enquiring mind. Tim has looked back from present times, through the nineteen fifties, when our addiction to the club began, to the years that came way before.

He has delved into the public record to trace the history of football in the county and has uncovered the early history of Gloucester City. He charts the determination of a small group of men who sought to bring the good news of association football to this benighted region.

Tim is a statistician, and quick to point that out. Nonetheless there are features of a narrative in *The Pioneers* and what's missing one can easily and pleasurably imagine. Did they settle down over a pint and a pipe to discuss plans for the club and team selection? I see them a bit like this, like an episode from Michael Palin's "Ripping Yarns".

This publication pays tribute to the pioneers and is also a tribute to its author. I sincerely hope that it will prove popular among Gloucester City supporters and that they will take pride in their club and its origins. I am sure that those in other parts of the footballing fraternity, especially perhaps those who follow the game at grass roots level, will be beguiled by the history Tim relates so thoroughly.

The Supporters' Trust at Gloucester City welcomes this highly significant history at a time when the ravages of the River Severn has threatened our very existence, causing us to abandon our home ground and find a tenancy in Forest Green.

The history that *The Pioneers* relates shows us how setbacks and struggles have been a part of the club from its earliest days. That we are still here today says a lot about our resolution and pride. May the pioneers' example, and that of Tim Clark too, lead us on into a bright new future.

Tim has determined that the profits from the sales of this publication will benefit the Trust. This is a very kind proposition, which we warmly welcome. Tim has some old-fashioned views about the way that games should be played and he puts a high value of good manners and sportsmanship. One can imagine that he would have been wholly at home with the pioneers and it is wonderful that he has shared their life and times with us.

Phil Warren
Chair
Gloucester City Supporters Trust

INTRODUCTION

"Lest We Forget"

I am not a writer I am a statistician. As anybody who knows me I am not a person to bask in the limelight of publicity so this task I undertook is done with all due humility.

With an entry in The Gloucester Journal that the formation of the first premier Gloucester club was 1883 it occurred to me that season 2007-2008 coincides with the 125th Anniversary so therefore it seemed appropriate to honour those players who pioneered football in this glorious city of Gloucester.

The week prior to Good Friday, 27th March 1959, I pestered my late Dad to take me to a football match and, bless him, he took me to see Gloucester City versus Lovells Athletic at Longlevens in a Southern League North West Division game. Unremarkable you might think but for the fact that my father was a 100% Rugby Union man and used to take me regularly to Kingsholm in the 1950s to the very spot his father used to take him in the 1920s. So you can imagine the wrench it must have been for him to take me to a football game on this Good Friday and to many more at the 'home of football' at that time. He must have been heart-broken! These are sacrifices fathers are prepared to take. I must confess, even today, along with Bobby Charlton and Rob Coldray, Mickey Booth is still a sporting hero of mine.

However, from this moment on I was a Gloucester City Supporter and joined the roller coaster that all true supporters endure.

My interest in collating information about Gloucester City Football Club started many years ago and I dabbled in and out, on and off, but unfortunately life just kept getting in the way. Living in London for many years it became difficult to watch as many games as I would like and playing football on a Saturday restricted my visits to Gloucester and I probably saw more of them away than I did at home during this period. But as I approached retirement I was able to spend a little more time on this project. The computer has been a real boon. Ideally, I would like all players who donned the City shirt to date to be recorded in some way or another but that is something to cogitate on. Maybe this publication is just a prelude to a mightier tome!

This is a publication of every Gloucester/Gloucester YMCA/Gloucester City player that there is still evidence of who participated in **LEAGUE FOOTBALL ONLY FROM 1893 TO 1914** and the corresponding League Tables.

Knowing that a Gloucester club first competed in an organised league, the Bristol and District League in 1893 this became my starting point. Imagine my amazement when the first league match a Gloucester team participated in contained a player named T.Clark. It was a sign that this was my destiny!

As far as I am aware all facts and figures are accurate but in the period this booklet celebrates many records and team selections are scarce and I was often left with just goal scorers or names mentioned in reports. In some cases it would have been easy to surmise who played in these missing matches but as a statistician I only deal in facts that are evident. However, I have used my discretion in obvious discrepancies. In some cases league tables do not add up or are incomplete because they were not published in full at the end of some seasons and, thus far, some organisations do not have this information. Although this is a record of League Football only, I have also recorded those players who appeared in other games. This means that 308 players altogether grace this booklet. These are the players that were at the forefront of football in Gloucester and players of which little is known.

Frustratingly in the early days there were always acres of information in The Citizen and The Journal about the Gloucester Rugby Football Club under the heading of 'football'! It emphasises the dominance of 'egg chasing' in those days and how difficult it was for football to get a footing in this fair City. But it was ever thus. Nothing has changed. Although judging by the number of football shirts you see worn around town you wonder why! Contentiously, Gloucester Rugby Club has always been our main rivals and not Cheltenham Town AFC. However, I believe there is room for all sports to co-exist in Gloucester.

It is highly unlikely that a publication of this sort is error free. It may be that my weary old eyes might have missed something. I take full responsibility. The mass of newspaper print that I scrutinised was daunting. A disastrous fire in 1946 destroyed many club records. Who knows what gems were lost forever? However, to repair the damage, I would be delighted to hear from anyone who has any information that would enhance the records of the club with regard to anything relating to this period including first names, birth or death dates and clubs played for by any of the players mentioned. Please write to me via the publishers address at the front of this book.

In 2010 we look forward to The Centenary of the present club. I hope you enjoy looking at this booklet as much as I did researching it. The way I look at it it's a start. Oh yes – and it's to help The Supporters Trust.

"clean up Our game" (see back page)

Love, Light and Peace,

Timothy RD Clark

ACKNOWLEDGEMENTS

Many thanks to the Gloucester Record Office in Alvin Street for allowing me so many hours searching primarily through the old Citizens and Gloucester Journals but also The Gloucestershire Chronicles, The Tewkesbury Register, The Dursley, Berkeley & Sharpness Gazette & Wotton-Under-Edge Advertiser, The Stroud News & Gloucester County Advertiser and The Gloucester Standard & Gloucestershire News. I would also like to thank Cheltenham Reference Library for allowing me access to The Gloucestershire Echo.

I would particularly like to thank The Citizen Newspaper for allowing me to use extracts from their newspaper during the period this booklet celebrates. Most of the line-ups in this book emanated from this newspaper.

Many thanks to Colin Timbrell, Historian, Gloucestershire Football Association who since 1994 has furnished me with league tables and other information about Gloucester football pre and post 1915.

The Internet has been a useful tool especially in finding some of the full names of players and birth dates. I would especially like to thank my elder brother, Ian Clark, who ploughed through the 1901 Census and other genealogical sites looking for birth years and places and for contributing other 'brilliant' suggestions.

A special thanks to Phil Warren, Chairman of the Supporters Trust for his co-operation and enthusiasm for this project.

I must also mention Jon Barnes of Gingerjonny Publications and author of 'The Who's Who of Grantham Town Football Club' who gave me some interesting tips in the ways of publishing.

I also have to thank my wife, Christine for her patience and my two boys, Paul (who is on the Supporters Trust Committee) and Simon (who writes match reports for the Under 18's for The Citizen) and both loyal T-Enders for encouraging me to take on such a task.

Note
The author would be pleased to hear from those who's copyright has been unintentionally infringed so as to avoid any further misuse in subsequent publications.
The author will not accept any responsibility for accuracy of content. Every effort was made to ensure accuracy.

Cover design by Simon Clark

Printing by am-pm design & print, 35 Slaney Street, Gloucester GL1 4TQ – Tel: (01452) 332027; Fax: (01452) 308911; e-mail: printing@am-pm.co.uk

Gloucester City Supporters Trust

The City Supporters Trust was formed in 2004 and born from the previous Supporters Club. It exists to support the future of Gloucester City AFC, but is also a representative body for the club's fans and seeks to ensure their views are heard at the very heart of the football club. The Trust seeks to make the club stronger, but the Trust itself is only as strong as the support it gets from members joining and supporting it through the giving of time and money. The Trust also has active support from national organisations and is a member of Supporters Direct and the Football Supporters Federation.

The Trust has clearly stated aims and has a long list of successes as by working together City fans have made sure the club has survived in some very difficult financial circumstances. See below for more details or read the Supporters Trust full constitution.

Following overwhelming support from its members at the August AGM Gloucester City Supporters Club has decided to adopt Trust status and the new company was launched on 12th November 2004 with a successful evening at Meadow Park.

The evening was well attended by City fans who were joined by local dignitaries, club directors, players, representatives of Supporters Direct and visiting fans from Merthyr Tydfil's own Trust. The meeting heard about the club's past and the hopes for the future from Trust Chairman Phil Warren who described how the Trust intended to work with the club to ensure it continued its 'bouncebackability' from financial crisis. He covered the previous success of the Supporters Club and pointed out that any other group who had raised such an extensive amount of money would be a story receiving huge publicity in the local media but the football club and supporters still had much to do to raise its profile in the city. The spirit and principles of the Supporters Club would pass on to the new Trust, which could now continue to grow in strength and influence.

There was a pledge of support from Gloucester MP Parmjit Dhanda who re-iterated his support for the club and the important role he believed it could play in the local community. Gloucester's Mayor, Cllr. Geraldine Gillespie, also pledged support for the club and wished it well as sport and the fans represent the city across the country. Fans were also addressed by representatives of Supporters Direct and national chairman Phil Tooley who explained some of the successes the movement has had at other clubs and made the point that fans were the only constant at a club, while directors and players came and went the fans remained and had a vital role to play.

The meeting then formally adopted the previous management committee of the Supporters Club appointed at the August AGM to become the new acting board of the Trust until it holds it's inaugural AGM next year. The point was made that the new board would welcome fans who wished to become involved, and also that much could be done to help the Trust without being part of the board. New acting Trust chairman Phil Warren thanked the four people who have done most to make the new Trust a reality and there was applause for Sandra Chase, Mike Dunstan, Judith Evans and Gwenda Halford.

With the formal part of the evening completed a celebratory Tiger cake was cut and fans were able to take advantage of an extensive buffet and chat about the future. Fans were also able to see the Trust's formal company plaque with registered company number which will now be placed on the club shop, the formal business address of the new Trust.

The Trust is ran by a Board elected democratically by the membership.
Two members of the Trust Board also represent fans' views on the executive committee that currently oversees the day-to-day running of Gloucester City AFC.

The Trust is also responsible for running the Club Shop and raising funds through the sale of merchandise.

The Trust raises enormous amounts of money to provide the club from everything from mowers for the pitch to bandages for the physio, as well as providing direct financial support to the first team and the youth team. All of this takes money, and the Trusts main financial cash flow is provided by regular monthly donations through the 500 club membership.

To get involved join the Supporters Trust or contact us for more details at any of the following:

Gloscity.trust@t-ender.co.uk

GCFC Supporters Trust, 8 Ivory Close, Tuffley, Gloucester GL4 0QY

Club Shop on match days.

(Reproduced with the permission of Paul Halford, www.t-ender.co.uk)

MAJOR GLOUCESTER CITY ASSOCIATION FOOTBALL CLUB WEBSITES:

www.gloucestercityafc.com

www.t-ender.co.uk

www.tigerroar.co.uk

EARLY YEARS OF GLOUCESTER CITY AFC 1883-1914

IN THE BEGINNING

It is hoped that the following conveys the struggle for a Gloucester association football team to get a foothold in this City. It is a paradox that the most popular sport in the country finds it difficult to make an impact on a population of over 110,000 in 2006. As you will see, it was ever thus. Rugby Union has become a religion in 'Glawster'. William Webb Ellis has a lot to answer for!

Before the 1870s, association football was looked upon as a form of exercise at public schools or a game between friends in a local park. However, with the administrative skills of gentlemen like Charles Alcock, Arthur Kinnaird, William McGregor and Francis Marindin the game grew to such an extent that it became an important part in the lives of both players and spectators as the century reached its conclusion.

Charles Alcock, Arthur Kinnaird, William McGregor and Francis Marindin

Gloucester was a contradiction to this growth. Following a meeting at the Spread Eagle Hotel in Gloucester on 15 September 1873 the Rugby Union club was established in the city. Initially, they played their home games at The Spa before moving to Kingsholm in 1891. By the time the association club was formed, Rugby Union had become well ensconced in the Gloucester sporting psyche.

The local newspaper, The Citizen, first appeared in 1876. Football was in its infancy and was still a struggling newcomer to the sporting scene. It was to be another seven years, before the first major City association football club came into being in March 1883.

Prior to 1883 the County had already produced the equivalent of today's soccer superstar. During his days at Eton and Oxford (1861-1869), Hubert Hastings Parry, of Highnam, was described as "the most brilliant football player of his time". He was to become renowned, not as a soccer player, but for his music, and his remains now lie in Saint Paul's Cathedral in London. However, there is no record of the great man donning the Gloucester shirt.

Hubert Parry

In 1949, Douglas Hunt, who was the Secretary-Manager of Gloucester City Association Football Club at the time, produced within the pages of a booklet to celebrate the Diamond Jubilee of the club an excellent history. He wrote that between March and October 1889, the Gloucester Association Club came into existence but of the inaugural meeting there was no record and it had been generally assumed that 1889 was the beginning of the club but the following entry in a local weekly newspaper disproved this.

The Gloucester Journal reported on 10 March 1883, that an Association Football Club had been formed in the city. This momentous event was announced as follows:
Gloucester Association Football Club – *A meeting of association players was held on Monday to consider the advisability of forming a club under association rules. The meeting was well attended, and a resolution was passed that a club should be formed, and the election of officers was forthwith proceeded with. Mr. W.H. Clarke, British School, was, appointed secretary. Already the club has enrolled 25 members.*

As The Gloucester Journal was dated from the Saturday, the exact date the Club was actually formed was on **Monday 5 March 1883** and so the current club is directly descended from this point. Therefore, it would appear that the Diamond Jubilee should have been celebrated in 1943 and not 1949!

Three years after this event, in 1886, the Gloucestershire Football Association was formed. A formation meeting was held in the Full Moon Hotel, Stokes Croft, Bristol on 7 September 1886. It's first President would be none other than Dr. W.G. Grace, the most dominant personality in Victorian cricket.

Even today there is some dispute as to when the club was formed. Looking through some away programmes from the late 1980s all begin their Gloucester City History - 'The Gloucester Journal reported in March 1883, that an association football club had been formed in the city....'.

Why was this fact dropped in favour of 1889 in future programmes? It would seem that the Club Directors were ready to celebrate The Centenary in 1989 when 1883 was unearthed and consequently the celebrations were abandoned as 1983 had passed.

In The Citizen Centenary Issue of 1976, an article quoted 1889 as the beginning of the club and even the Wealdstone Southern League Cup Final programme of 1982 has 1889. Therefore, for a short period of time during the 1980s and early 1990s, 1883 was recognised and seemingly dropped.

Although 1883 is a significant year in the history of the club, the coming together of the Reverend Henry Lloyd Brereton and Mr. Charles Frederick Poole a couple of years later was most influential, with their enthusiasm for the association game. It is important to note that the clergy loomed large in the beginnings of many football clubs during the Victorian era and Gloucester was no different. It seemed an ideal sport to provide boys with a sense of discipline, moral values and responsibility.

The first newspaper recorded match by a team known as Gloucester was in a friendly against Eastville Rovers (now known as Bristol Rovers) on 2 January 1886, being beaten 0-1 in Bristol. Their defeat was followed by their first Junior Cup win at Budding's Field – not a stone's throw from the Horton Road Stadium site of the 1960s. However, in a book entitled 'Bristol Rovers – The Definitive History 1883-2003' by Stephen Byrne and Mike Jay there is reference to a Gloucester team playing Eastville Rovers in 1884-1885, date and result unknown.

Where exactly was Budding's Field? On the 1851 Census, it indicates that a George Budding of Union Lane, Gloucester was a farmer with 12 acres of land, which was situated within the area of what is London Road and Great Western Road in the vicinity of the Gloucester Union Workhouse, which became the old Gloucester Infirmary. Mr. Budding's surname was thus adopted for this plot of land. Budding's Field was located at the end of Claremont Road through to Great Western Road (i.e. The Hyde and/or City Stone Ground). This is the area opposite Alvin Street and alongside Great Western Road.

In the Centenary Supplement of The Citizen of 1 May 1976, an article entitled 'When Bare Knees Were Shocking' had the following:
The real pioneers of the game in the immediate area were the Assistant Head of the Crypt School, Mr. Charles Poole, and The Reverend H.L. Brereton, Hempsted County School's Headmaster, both Cambridge men.
At the end of his first season in 1886, Mr. Brereton reported a problem that is still very noticeable today [1976] – *that of re-educating boys in Association rules after being so long accustomed to the Rugby Code*
The article continued:
The game was in a state of continuing change in all its aspects. Throw-ins were actually kicked in, at first by the player retrieving the ball and later by the man who kicked it out!
With no goal area, kicks were taken from the goal line, and handling was still permitted, to stop the ball and place it at the feet. Any attacker in front of the ball was out of play (off side) and not until 1878 was the first referee's whistle heard.
Previously the game was controlled by one, or sometimes two, flag-waving umpires on the side lines. The change from knee-breeches to shorts created the first public outcry against the game. When players ran too fast they "embarrassed the ladies present by exposing the knee-cap." "Shocking", "indecent" and "most unseemly", said the ladies.

As the Reverend Brereton intimated from those early days, the Club has been fighting a continuous battle for survival in an area dominated by Rugby Football and 125 years later, nothing has changed. Gloucester would appear to be a desert for 'the beautiful game'.

Henry Lloyd Brereton was a soccer enthusiast and came to Gloucester to become headmaster of the new County School at Hempsted whose magazine, the "Glo'strian" contains early records of soccer in Gloucester. He was 23-years old and the son of Joseph Lloyd Brereton, an educational reformer. He was aided and abetted by 27-year-old Charles Frederick Poole, who was the assistant headmaster at the Crypt Grammar School. As already mentioned pupils at this time were not versed in Association Football but it would be these two men who would pioneer soccer in Gloucester and, indeed, don the Gloucester shirt themselves.

For the season 1887-88 the Editor of the Glo'strian said:
During the autumn term we were as unsuccessful at football as we had been at cricket; a fact that may be due to our having adopted association rules and our boys having been accustomed to Rugby Union rules.
The following season, a more optimistic view was in evidence:
We have improved, but the Association rules are coming steadily in favour round about, and we have to play teams who work well together and have improved even more than ourselves since last year.

With the popularity of Association Football seemingly on the rise the time seemed ripe to re-form a premier Gloucester club once again.

RE-FORMED 1

The fact that the first recorded match was in 1886 pre-supposes that the club was formed before that. However, in The Gloucester Journal of Saturday 14 September 1889 it was announced:
Formation of an Association Club in Gloucester – *At a meeting convened at the Ram Hotel on Tuesday evening* [10 September 1889] *by Messrs. A.S. King and W. Sessions it was unanimously*

decided to form an Association football club, to be called "The Gloucester Association Football Club". Mr. C.F. Poole was elected captain, Mr. W. Sessions sub-captain, Mr.A.S. King, of Theresa-place, Gloucester, secretary and treasurer, and the committee consisted of the foregoing and Messrs. S. Wade, W.A.S. Ely, T.B. Powell, F. Platt, H.G. Brown and F. Fielding. It was announced that Budding's Field had been secured for the season, and it was decided that practice commence on Saturday, the 21st inst. Black and White were selected for the colours of the team, and the subscription was fixed at 5s. It was announced that fixtures had been arranged with Clifton, Warmley and Worcester Rovers (two each) and that negotiations were pending with Swindon Town, Hereford Town, Hereford College, Ledbury and others. It was resolved that the club be entered for the Gloucestershire Challenge Cup Competition. About 30 members have already joined the club.

The Ram & County Hotel,
GLOUCESTER.

Between this announcement and the one in 1883 might suggest that the earlier club folded. There is no official record of disbandment but the following in The Gloucester Journal of Saturday 10 November 1888 is the only clue to its demise:

We notice that one or two Association clubs are springing into existence in Gloucester besides those in connection with some of the public schools here. There was once a Gloucester team who played under these rules, but the club died, we presume from inanition and lack of public support. Still, as there seems to be a growing interest in the game, the present might be an opportune time for the resurrection of a city club. Although the Rugby code has a strong hold on the affections of the football loving public it might be worth while once more trying if the twin game cannot command a share of attention in the city. To create a demand for the game, however, a supply of good exponents must be forthcoming; but we make a presentation gratis, of this suggestion to local Association players.

Therefore, it would appear the original club disbanded due to lack of vitality or spirit.

It cannot be underestimated the influence of the Crypt Grammar School and the County School during these formative years. In a match between these two schools on 23 March 1889, no less than 14

participants (9 from the Crypt and 5 from the County) were to play in the early Gloucester teams. The most outstanding of all Crypt sportsmen was Graham Wilshaw Parker and he played for Gloucester City during the late 1920s. A master at Crypt School, Mr. J.L. Somerville would captain the club in 1892-93. Indeed, the Crypt link carries on to this day with Tom Webb.

Certainly, the fixtures began in earnest from 1889. The club's opening game of the 1889-90 season on 5 October 1889, Clifton beat Gloucester on Ashley Down, Bristol, but the game was significant because none other than the legendary Gloucestershire and England cricketer, DR. W.G. GRACE, refereed it. For this season it would have cost you 'tuppence' to watch Gloucester play.

The aforementioned match was reported as follows:
'The chief characteristic of the team was the youthfulness of the players. Of the three Chadborn brothers, the eldest was only 19.
F.B. Fielding, Walter Sessions and, it's believed, A.Gardner were also in their teens. R.D. Wade, the curate of Hartpury, must have been older.
Compared with these lads, the bearded captain, Frederick Poole, of the Crypt School, was still in his prime. He was the first Gloucester player to play for his county, and his death in Jamaica, a few years later, caused great regret.
On the County Ground at Ashley Down, Dr. W.G. Grace was waiting to officiate as referee, and for the absent goalkeeper, Murch, the groundsman, acted as substitute.
The crowd was not as large as usual. To quote the Bristol Times and Mirror: 'Probably the followers of Association knew that Gloucester were weak, and did not wish to witness a one-sided contest.' [The game was also reported in the Gloucester Journal and the Western Daily Press].
By half-time Gloucester were two goals down – not a bad position when one considers the strength of their opponents.
During the second half the team had begun to tire, and so completely was play confined to the Gloucester territory that while Pearce, on the Clifton right-wing was receiving treatment for injury, Bush, the home keeper, lit his pipe and was able to smoke during the remainder of the game.
Four more goals raised the Clifton total to six, while Gloucester failed to score.
The [Gloucester] backs, with their fine clearances, came in for favourable mention. The half-backs were good, but Walter Sessions did not keep in his place, and very often was seen playing in front of the forwards.
Wade, King, E.N. Chadburn and F. Fielding, played a fine passing game, but when it came to shooting they were failures.'

Before league football was introduced to Gloucester, there was not much serious competition and, once knocked out of cup competitions, there was little to offer the spectators other than friendly games or Challenge games as they used to call them. Friendlies therefore during this period 1883 to 1914 had more significants that they do nowadays.

Frustratingly there is nary a mention of the Club in either The Citizen or The Journal during the 1880s, reinforcing the lack of interest in the association game in Gloucester. Indeed, The Gloucester Journal called association football supporters, rather dismissively, 'The Associationists'.

At the end of the 1889-90 season, The Gloucester Journal of Saturday 5 April 1890 summed up the season:
The Gloucester Association Football Club was established at the beginning of this season, and considering the difficulties which a club of necessity meets with in its infancy, and especially so when introducing a game comparatively new to the district, the season has been one of success. The most formidable difficulty which the club has had to contend with has been that of securing anything like the same eleven to do battle throughout the season. No less than 36 men have filled positions in the first eleven, and on no two occasions have the teams been identically the same. This will, no doubt, be

remedied as the game is better appreciated and each member takes a more enthusiastic interest in it. The difficulty will have to be faced, however, so long as the club is not in a position to pay the expenses of the team in out matches.

There were no competitive fixtures in season 1890-91 in which Gloucester completed 20 friendly games. At the end of this season, The Gloucester Journal of Saturday 28 March 1891 remarked:
We are glad to be able to congratulate such a young body as the Gloucester Association Football Club on a successful season's work...
Of course the fact that there have been so many variations in the team [42 personnel] has told against combination; but had the club sufficient cash receipts to justify the payment of members' expenses an improvement might be looked for in these respects. What the prospects of the club for next year are it is difficult to say, but there is very substantial encouragement in the present season's record.
During this season, George Speck made his debut in goal. It was felt he was the best Gloucester 'keeper during this period in their history. He was acclaimed as a legend in later years by followers of Association Football in Gloucester.

In 1891-92 the club entered the Gloucestershire Senior Cup but were knocked out in the first round by Bristol Saint George's at Budding's Field losing 3-4. The Gloucester Journal of Saturday 12 March 1892 opined:
The Gloucester Association Football Club is showing very poor form indeed this season.
The review of the season in The Gloucester Journal of Saturday 7 May 1892 read as follows:
Association football does not seem to enjoy anything approaching the popularity which the Rugby game has obtained in Gloucester and perhaps will not until the "Socker" men achieve some distinct notoriety in the field. All things considered the Gloucester Association Football Club have reason to be congratulated upon their record for the season just ended. Out of fourteen matches played seven were won, five lost and two drawn, and in "analyzing" this it must be remembered that the club has suffered more during the season than at any period of its existence from continued changes and absenteeism, the services of no less than 37 players having been requisitioned to represent the eleven. It is hoped that the team will make themselves more prominent next year and that the players will be able to play more regularly.

On 24 September 1892, The Gloucestershire Chronicle reported:
Gloucester Association Club would be in existence during the winter and would be much stronger than ever, as several good players have joined. The season will open with a balance of over £6 in hand, which has gradually accumulated from previous years, and when it is considered that the Club does not receive its fair share of public patronage at its matches, such a balance is highly satisfactory.

The season of 1892-93 brought Gloucester their first brush with honours. They reached the final of The Gloucestershire Senior Cup only to lose at the Chequers Ground in Kingswood against Warmley by 1-4 in front of 3,000 to 4,000 people. En route to this final they beat Bedminster at Budding's Field 5-0 in the Semi-Final attracting a gate receipt of £20. The following season Gloucester were to test themselves by entering a league for the very first time.

LEAGUE FOOTBALL COMMENCES
In 1893, Gloucester entered the Bristol and District League, which subsequently became the Western League in 1895. It was to be hoped that the more competitive nature of the games would draw extra enthusiasm toward the association game in Gloucester.

In The Citizen of Friday 29 September 1893, the first team to represent Gloucester Football Club in a League match was announced as follows:
Gloucester v Bedminster – The following team will represent Gloucester at Bristol tomorrow in their opening League fixture:- Kent, goal; J.L.Somerville, R.N.Green, backs; Rev.J.Harvey, H.H.Scott,

T.Clark, half-backs; W.Matthews, H.T.Robins (right wing), F.B.Fielding (centre), H.G.Sherwood, P.W.Stout (left wing), forwards. Train leaves at 1:28.

The Citizen the following day (Saturday, 30 September 1893) reported the match thus:
The Gloucester Association XI journeyed to Bristol on Saturday to try conclusions with Bedminster, this being their first match in the Bristol and District League Competition. About 1,500 spectators witnessed the game, which was very evenly contested; and though Gloucester were the losers by three goals to two, they had quite as much of the game as their opponents. Bedminster were lucky to obtain a lead of two goals in the first half, as the Gloucester backs with both wind and sun in their faces scored against their own side. After the interval Bedminster quickly added their third goal, but from now to the finish the home team had to act mainly on the defensive. Stout and Fielding both scored for Gloucester, in each case after some good play. The visitors tried hard to get on equal terms, but the Bedminster backs managed to prevent any further score.

------------------***---------------

On Saturday's form Gloucester are fortunate to secure a good goal-keeper in Kent. As back Somerville was at his best, heading and kicking splendidly. Green and Harvey also put in a lot of good work. Fielding and Stout were the pick of the forwards, but the combination of the five was upset by the loss of Sherwood early in the game owing to a strained leg. This no doubt materially affected the result. Seeing that Gloucester have not played together before this season, and that their opponents are one of the strongest in the League, the city eleven have no reason to be discouraged with the result of their first League match.

------------------***---------------

Referring to the match the "Bristol Mercury" cannot help thinking that Gloucester are capable of a much higher standard than that which they reached on Saturday.
Gloucester disappointed everybody, says the "Times and Mirror." It was expected they would be handicapped by the loss of Speck's services in goal, but Kent proved a worthy substitute. Indeed with Somerville, Fielding and Stout he alone did anything to maintain the reputation of the club. Green was very unreliable, while the halves, probably from lack of training were quite at sea, being unable to check the opposing forwards or feed their own even when they had the ball. Some excuse can be made for the forwards, because a couple got injured. At times they showed excellent passing, and Stout's goal was the result of a fine bit of dribbling. Though beaten, the team ought to come out very well in the League, for they have as good a back in Somerville as could be found in the county. Fielding is also a thoroughly useful centre, while Stout is a most reliable man. Saturday's defeat should therefore not discourage them; on the contrary, it should teach them their weaknesses, which might be remedied by the time of the next match.

Also, in this first season in League football, the City club used Kingsholm for one of the games. The game was against Eastville Rovers on 11 November 1893. Apparently, it was not unusual in the past for the Club to use the facilities of the Rugby team but only if a Rugby match was abandoned. This match was unusual because it was advertised from over a week before and was the first and only league match advertised for Kingsholm. The Citizen of Saturday 11 November 1893 reported it thus:
The local Association club were favoured in local circumstances today to a degree of its history. It has before reaped advantage by the abandonment of the counter Rugby attraction at the last moment but on the present occasion, the fixture with Eastville Rovers had been billed for more than a week as the great football attraction....
Gloucester won 3-0 before an attendance of 700, which during this period was a record for a home Gloucester league match. This figure was surpassed when Gloucester met Eastville Rovers again in a Gloucestershire Senior Cup Semi-Final match on 24 February 1894 when 1,000 attended at Budding's Field. Unfortunately, Gloucester lost 0-1. Gloucester City used Kingsholm once more during this period against Ross Town in a Gloucester and District League match on 3 March 1900 winning 3-2. It is interesting to note that the Rugby club also shared Kingsholm with the Gloucester Hockey Club.

Worcester Street early 1900s

On 10 March 1894, Gloucester played a game against a Mr. J. Hanman's XI which was effectively the Gloucester Rugby Club. This match was arranged because at the time the Rugby Club had been suspended for a month by the Rugby Union and as Bedminster had to cancel their fixture with the Gloucester Association Club due to replaying a cup-tie a match was arranged at Budding's Field between the two Gloucester Clubs, the Rugby eleven being captained by Mr. J. Hanman. The Gloucester Journal of 17 March 1894 reported:
The novelty of the encounter attracted a moderate sized crowd to Budding's Field, and if the exhibition which resulted was not an ideal exposition of the Association game, it certainly proved a capital practice for the "suspenders" while the coffers of the Association Club received a much needed lift. The scratch eleven displayed creditable form, considering several of the players had never taken part in a 'soccer' game before. Bagwell, W. Collins, Taylor, and J. Partridge especially distinguished themselves. At half time the association team had scored three goals to one, and in the concluding portion the leaders added three more. A.H. Click shot the goal for the scratch after some clever passing, and F. Fielding was responsible for three goals for the winners. J.A. Franklin kept goal in capital style for the losers and cleared several dangerous shots."
The Gloucestershire Chronicle adds:
The Play was more amusing than scientific as some of the Rugbyites could not or would not accustom themselves to the difference in the style of play. They were continually penalised for picking up the ball with their hands instead of using their heads and their feet. However, some of the Rugby players put in bits of good play. Taylor, James, and the brothers Click exhibiting perhaps the best form."

For the 1895-96 season, Gloucester moved to the Avenue Road Ground in Tuffley Avenue from Budding's Field. The Citizen of 20 September 1895 reported:
…Committee of the Club indulge in the hope that the new ground with its stands and appurtenances will lead to an extension of the patronage given by the public in past years.
It is believed the players used to change in the Avenue Hotel which still exists today on the corner of Tuffley Avenue and Bristol Road.

Avenue Hotel

A major smallpox epidemic in Gloucester late 1895 and early 1896 would have affected all sport in the city. To put the epidemic into perspective of 541 deaths from smallpox in England and Wales in 1896, 443 occurred in the registration district of Gloucester. Children were moved from the union workhouse in Great Western Road to Tuffley leaving the city virtually in quarantine. For a club that led a fragile existence financially the epidemic would certainly have serious consequences.

An example of financial constraints is demonstrated by their withdrawal from the English Amateur Cup. The Citizen of 11 October 1895 reported thus:
The Gloucester Association team which was drawn to play Bournemouth in the English Amateur Cup Competition tomorrow have conceded the tie to the Southerners, since the latter could guarantee anything to Gloucester for their expenses nor hold out any prospect of a "gate". Since the expenses attendant on the journey would have been considerable the Gloucester executive have not felt justified in incurring the liability, and consequently the first team have a rest.

A further example of difficulties during this 1895-96 season was reported in The Gloucester Journal of Saturday 9 May 1896:
At a meeting of the Western League, held on Wednesday in reference to the unplayed matches, Swindon Wanderers v Gloucester and Bedminster v Gloucester, it was resolved that the games should be considered drawn and each club given one point.
The following Saturday The Gloucester Journal printed the Gloucester response:
The tardy award by the Western District League in respect of unplayed matches in the competition (two of which were due to the reluctance of teams to visit Gloucester) determines the position of the city eleven in the table as that of sixth. Bearing in mind the misfortunes of the Club this is highly creditable, for it was only with the greatest difficulty that the Club fulfilled all its engagements.
With the implied difficulties, it is hardly surprising that the club folded. Gloucester withdrew from The Western League at the end of season 1895-96 due to financial problems. Nothing changes!

The Western Daily Press of 31 August 1896 pronounced:
The withdrawal of Gloucester is hardly a surprise, but it is at the same time attended with much regret, as the 'Cestrians had always evinced a true love of sport, and though at great personal expense and of time at equal inconvenience, they have loyally kept their fixtures, whether out or at home, and moreover their ranks have frequently furnished men to the teams that have played as representing the Bristol district against more powerful professional organizations from the North and the Midlands. Particularly was this the case last season, when it will be remembered that Percy Stout, who it is stated is about to leave England, and Frank Fielding, practically won the match against 'Aston Villa', which will always be regarded as one of the best, if not the best, achievement of local Association players.

During this first incursion into league football, the brothers Stout, Percy and Frank loomed large. In fact in The Gloucester Journal of Saturday 25 July 1896 the following was printed:
Percy Stout, one of the best, if not quite the very best centre-forward ever called upon to wear the black and white shirt of the Gloucestershire Football Association....
Both Percy and Frank Stout went on to play Rugby for Gloucester and represented England in 5 and 7 Internationals respectively. Both were former Cryptians continuing the schools links with the club. Also at this time, Gilbert Jessop, the legendary Gloucestershire and England cricketer and team mate of W.G. Grace was to play a few games for the Gloucester football team.

Gilbert Jessop

Certainly, during the Victorian era and perhaps upto World War One without the Railway it would have been impossible to have such a diverse league. It would have been unlikely one could have got to those far-flung places like Trowbridge and Bristol without the train. Many of the players were working men probably working a six-day week with jobs as diverse as Clergymen, Fitters, Surveyors, Labourers, Mill Hands and Teachers.

Although Gloucester had withdrawn from the Western League at the end of the 1895-96 season due to the aforementioned financial problems, in 1896-97 Gloucester still continued playing. They played 16 Friendly games. For the last two seasons, Gloucester had been running at a loss and were very much in the doldrums. The Citizen of Tuesday 22 September 1896 included the following:
...*However, on Monday evening a well-attended meeting of members held at Gloucester Hotel under the presidency of Mr. H.H. Scott (last year's captain) resolved that the club should be carried on through another season. It was determined that the offer of the joint use with the Post Office Club of the Co-operative field in India-road should be accepted on the terms arranged. Mr. W.H. Godby, jun., was unanimously elected captain and Mr. Walter Hicks vice-captain.*

With the withdrawal from any league competition, local interest, which was apathetic anyway, evaporated. At the AGM in 1897, a more positive outlook for the future of the club was voiced with the prospect of League football returning but on a more local scale. Revival was in the air. It was felt that keeping the fixtures local would alleviate the financial burden of traveling. At a meeting in the Albion Hotel on July 5 1897, representatives from interested parties unanimously decided to form a League. These included Gloucester, Cheltenham Town, Tewkesbury Abbey, Ross Kyrle, Price Walkers, Cavendish House and Saint Michael's School.

The 1897-98 season saw the Gloucester and District League inaugurated and Gloucester became one of its founder members, winning the Championship at the first attempt. They repeated this feat in 1899-1900. Gloucester had also returned to Budding's Field for one season only resuming back to the Avenue Road Ground for the 1898-99 season. It should also be noted that the first team competed in the Mid Gloucestershire League for 1898-99 to 1900-1901, to fill out what was a very skimpy Gloucester and District League fixture list.

In many reports in The Citizen at this time, the Gloucester football team were described as 'The Citizens' and, on occasions, 'The Gloucestrians'.

Prior to the 1898-99 season, The Citizen of Saturday 27 August 1898, seemed to be in positive mode:
The Gloucester Association Club open their season on October 1st with most encouraging prospects; in fact, the future outlook for the dribbling game was never so bright in the city as at present. The City

Club have again taken the Avenue Ground for the season, and though the enclosure is hardly so central as one could wish, it certainly affords far better accommodation for both spectators and players than the old ground at Budding's Field.
No doubt the great drawback, as regards the Association game in Gloucester, has been the lack of support accorded by the public. Amateurism, in its true sense, has always been the Club's motto, but still there is always considerable expense attached to a club of this description which can only be met by the cordial support of all lovers of sport. The Club, as becomes the premier Association team of the city, has an earnest desire to foster the game amongst the schools, and with this object in view they have placed their ground at the disposal of the Schools' Association Football League. This League should form a splendid nursery for the premier club, but the youngsters should not be lost sight of after leaving school.
The Reverend Brereton and Mr. Poole no doubt would have been delighted.

RE-FORMED II: GLOUCESTER CITY

At the end of 1900-01 season, Gloucester did not apply to join the Gloucester and District League. The Diamond Jubilee booklet intimated the reason could only have been the difficulty of finding officials and was not financial. The players of Gloucester City at this time were men in good positions and of some standing in the district. They gladly paid their own expenses, and were willing to help the club in every way.

It was during this season that there was a two-week break because of the death of 'our beloved Queen (Victoria)' who had reigned for nigh on sixty years. At a Gloucester and District League meeting of 24 August 1901, the League secretary announced that it had definitely been decided that there would be no Gloucester club in the ensuing season. The Gloucester Pioneer Club were willing to enter the First Division as the major city club if it could recruit the Gloucester players. This was declined.

In 1902, 'City' was officially added to the Gloucester title, although the first mention in The Citizen of the team being called Gloucester City was when the team was printed on Friday 16 November 1900 for the Mid Gloucestershire League game at home to Brimscombe the following day. The Club returned to Budding's Field and competed in the Gloucester and District League for 1902-03 and 1903-04 when it was disbanded yet again. The 1902-03 season was a brilliant one for the City winning the Gloucestershire FA Junior Cup Final against Warmley 3-1 at the Chequers Ground, Kingswood on 26 December 1902 in front of 1,000 people. It was the first time this cup left Bristol.

A stalwart of the Club from the very first League game of 1893 was Arthur Fielding who was still going strong in 1904. If Gloucester City had a 'Hall of Fame' he surely would be in it. So would his elder brother, Frank, who also gave great service to the club from 1889 to 1899. However, their beloved Gloucester City team went into the wilderness for two seasons.

RE-FORMED III: AMALGAMATION

The Club amalgamated with the Hempsted team of Saint Michael's prior to the start of season 1906-07. The 'new' Gloucester City competed again in the Gloucester and District League but the first team also entered the Cheltenham and District League in 1906-07, winning the Championship at the first attempt. Again, as in seasons before the added league was entered in order to fill out the fixture list.

In The Citizen of 23 September 1906, the advent of a new season was reported thus:
Soccer football is going to boom in Gloucester once more. The resuscitation of the city teams has proved a popular move, and there appears a general desire on the part of the players and supporters of the game to make the Club a big success, and one worthy of the name Gloucester City.
The old St. Michael's Club is practically merged into the new organisation, so that some valuable players and officials were at once available. In addition, St. Luke's Club has ceased to exist, which still further strengthens the playing strength of Gloucester.

The black shirts, with white sleeves and neckband, which had been the City colours for so long, yielded to the red and white stripes of Saint Michaels.

At the end of this season, The Citizen of 13 April 1907 printed a review of the season which went thus: *Gloucester City – A successful season – The first season of the City club (late Saint Michael's) must be regarded with the utmost satisfaction. Reviewing all the circumstances connected with the inauguration of a "premier" club, it would not have been surprising if the first year had been unsuccessful. As a "local" institution Saint Michael's had made rapid advances: but there is such a thing as a local club running to the end of its tether, and it was recognized that a City combination would offer greater possibilities for the advancement of soccer in Gloucester and the district. The disbanding of the old City team provided the necessary opportunity, and this was seized; but it was early evident that the formation and successful running of a premier club involved much increased responsibility. For instance, an enclosed ground is necessary for purposes of gate, and this entailed a big advance in rent. Many features presented themselves which might prove of stumbling blocks to success and not a few of Saint Michael's supporters deplored the spirit of those whose motto was "Excelsior".*
That the fears of the critics were groundless is amply demonstrated in the results of the first season's working. In the first place a strong and capable committee was elected, the energetic hon. Secretary (Mr. J.E. Palmer) again consented to take office, and several old City players and supporters gave their services and sympathy to the undertaking. Both from the points of view of finance and play, the club has met with great success. It is impossible now to state exactly how the income will figure as against expenditure, but there is no doubt that when these matters are settled a fairly substantial balance on the right side will be shown by the Treasurer.

In The Citizen of 23 March 1907, there was mention of advancement of football in Gloucestershire with the inauguration of the North Gloucestershire League. Gloucester City became one of its founder members joining in 1907-08 to 1909-10 being Champions on the first two occasions.

THE END IS NIGH

This was a time of unsettlement and of general uncertainty within the club. The Citizen of 10 October 1908 recorded after the match against Midlands & South Western Junction Railway that:
The contest provided some interesting football but the attendance of onlookers was very scanty. Amateur Association football does not seem to rouse Gloucestrians to enthusiasm.

However, when they did get a reasonable crowd the excitement was tangible. The Citizen of 16 January 1909 after the visit of Swindon Town Reserves to Budding's Field commented:
Considering the lamentable lack of interest which Gloucestrians display where Association football is concerned, there was a fair crowd at Budding's Field on Saturday and the takings at the gate fell little short of £3. We are in a position to contradict the rumour that when this total was announced by him who sat at the receipt of tolls, an awesome hush was only broken by the tense and solitary query – "Is there so much money in the world?"

Gloucester City participated yet again in the Cheltenham and District League in 1909-10 to, as in previous seasons, bulk up a thin fixture list.
The Citizen of 12 March 1910 reported about the perilous position the club were in:
The present condition of the Gloucester Association Football Club's finances is a parlous one. In other words, their funds are very low. Now this is not as it should be.
It must be remembered that at the beginning of this season the club joined the Cheltenham League, in addition to the North Gloucestershire. This was done in the hope that League matches might attract a bigger gate than mere friendlies. Somehow or other Gloucestrians seem half-hearted about the Association game; yet there must be a good following of interested local sportsmen.

In addition to this arrangement, Mr. Carter, to whose work in the capacity of hon. Secretary the Club owes much, did all in his power to prevent the clashing of his Association home fixture with the Rugby ones.
These efforts proved unable to secure for the Club an increased income. It must however, be remembered that a very wet February, changes in programme due to County Intermediate Cup fixtures and a regrettable falling off in the team's strength, have mitigated against a successful season.

The writing was on the wall. Even a whist drive was arranged toward the end of the season and it was thought players could only subscribe so much. After the friendly game away to Swindon Town Reserves on Saturday 17 March 1910, The Citizen of 26 March 1910 printed an extract from the Swindon Borough programme which is worthy of quoting:
"Association football has had a terrible struggle in Gloucester with the Rugger code, and at various times it has been in danger of extinction, but it has survived, and there may yet be a first-class team in the Cathedral City. The team is purely amateur, but they have some promising men. Association football is making inroads in South Wales, and there will be a strong team in Cardiff next season. Whether this will give Soccer an impetus in the surrounding district remains to be seen. Gloucester people should take the opportunity of seeing a few first-class Association games, and then they would see more in it than they apparently do at the present."

At the end of the 1909-10 season, Gloucester City disbanded again. Financial difficulties finally ended the club. There is mention in the Gloucester Citizen of Tuesday 30 August 1910 of a portion of Budding's Field being sold. It reads:
Budding's Field: The following letter was received from the Local Government Board:-
"I am directed by the Local Government Board to advert to your letter of the 3rd inst., and with reference to the proposed sale by the Guardians of the Gloucester Union of a portion of their land known as Budding's Field..."
Given the circumstances, it is entirely possible that this was the demise of the ground that Gloucester City had used 16 out of 23 seasons since the 1880s.

On Saturday 3 September 1910, the following article appeared in The Citizen:
The announcement that the Gloucester City Association Club has been disbanded was received with regret by the local followers of the Soccer code. It is four years since the club was formed out of the old St. Michael's and the first three seasons were as successful as could be desired.
Last year, however, the team had bad luck to begin with. After two or three reverses some of the players allowed their interest to flaw and it was often only with great difficulty that the club managed to put a team into the field at all.
A number of members still owe their subscriptions, and the club is in debt; several officers and players have sent in their resignations and Budding's Field is not obtainable this season. These depressing facts have been followed by their inevitable sequel – disbandment.

RE-FORMED IV: GLOUCESTER YMCA
Coincidentally, the Gloucester YMCA club was formed in 1910. This club after World War One would have a significant role in the resurrection of Gloucester City Association Football Club. Initially, the YMCA club competed in the minor Gloucester and District Thursday League.

The coincidence can hardly be discounted and it would be difficult not to suggest that Gloucester YMCA were Gloucester City in disguise from 1910. They were the senior club in Gloucester at the time and although previous club history's had 'adopted' them only from 1919 onward the 1910 formation of this club would appear to make more sense.

After discussions with Rob Kujawa (Gloucester City Historian) and Colin Timbrell (Gloucestershire FA Historian) it was concluded based on the criteria of a continuous link on a seasonal basis that the current club could claim they were formed in 1910. However, the link with all the clubs going back to the 1883 formation is irrefutable.

The YMCA club continued in the lesser Gloucester and District Thursday League between 1910 and 1913 but it decided to enter a team in the North Gloucestershire League Division Two in 1913-1914 as the senior Gloucester team and at least three former City players appeared for them.

When the First World War ended many of the men who were later to be identified with City, attached themselves to Gloucester YMCA. To all intents and purposes, it would be City competing under a different banner and it would be 1925 that the YMCA merged into a Gloucester City club.

With the advent of World War One, many of the past and present Gloucester footballers were called up or volunteered to serve their country. The future was uncertain.

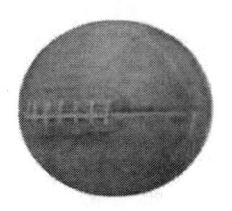

LEAGUE FOOTBALL

1893-1914

ALTHOUGH A GLOUCESTER ASSOCIATION FOOTBALL CLUB WAS FORMED ON MONDAY 5 MARCH 1883 A GLOUCESTER CLUB DID NOT PARTICIPATE IN LEAGUE FOOTBALL UNTIL 30 SEPTEMBER 1893 IN THE BRISTOL AND DISTRICT LEAGUE.

1893-1894 – BRISTOL AND DISTRICT LEAGUE – FIRST DIVISION
(Gloucester played at Budding's Field).

30/09/1893 v BEDMINSTER (A) Lost 2-3   Att: 1,500
SJF Kent; JL Somerville, RN Green; Rev. JH Harvey, HH Scott, T Clark; WG Matthews, HT Robins, FB Fielding, HG Sherwood, PW Stout.
Scorers: Stout, Fielding.

14/10/1893 v EASTVILLE ROVERS (A) Lost 2-5   Att: 200-300
SJF Kent; JL Somerville, RN Green; HH Scott, Rev. JH Harvey, ? Pennington; HT Robins, HG Sherwood, PW Stout, AF Fielding, FB Fielding.
Scorer: Stout, Robins.
(This was the first game played at the new Eastville ground)

28/10/1893 v SAINT GEORGE (A) Won 3-0
SJF Kent; JL Somerville, RN Green; AC Cragg, HH Scott, Rev. JH Harvey; HT Robins, EF Stebbing, FB Fielding, HG Sherwood, PW Stout.
Scorer: Stout (3).

04/11/1893 v STAPLE HILL (H) Drew 1-1
SJF Kent; JL Somerville, RN Green; AC Cragg, HH Scott, Rev. JL Harvey; HT Robins, EF Stebbing, FB Fielding, Wilfred Sessions, PW Stout.
Scorer: Stebbing.

11/11/1893 v EASTVILLE ROVERS (H, Kingsholm) Won 3-0   Att: 700
SJF Kent; JL Somerville, RN Green; AC Cragg, HH Scott, Rev. JL Harvey; HT Robins, EF Stebbing, FB Fielding, HG Sherwood, PW Stout.
Scorers: Sherwood, Robins, Stout.

18/11/1893 v CLEVEDON (H) Won 2-1
SJF Kent; JL Somerville, RN Green; FM Stout, HH Scott, AC Cragg; HT Robins, EF Stebbing, FB Fielding, HG Sherwood, PW Stout.
Scorers: Sherwood, Stebbing.

02/12/1893 v CLIFTON (H) Won 2-0
SJF Kent; JL Somerville, AC Cragg; FM Stout, HH Scott, Rev. JH Harvey; HT Robins, WG Matthews,
FB Fielding, HG Sherwood, PW Stout.
Scorers: Sherwood, Matthews.

16/12/1893 v TROWBRIDGE TOWN (H) Lost 1-3
SJF Kent; JL Somerville, RN Green; FM Stout, HH Scott, AC Cragg; HT Robins, Rev. JH Harvey,
FB Fielding, HG Sherwood, PW Stout.
Scorer: PW Stout.

23/12/1893 v MANGOTSFIELD (A) Lost 1-3
SJF Kent; FM Morris, HH Scott; AC Cragg, Walter Sessions, AE Johnson; HT Robins, FM Stout,
A Jessop, HG Sherwood, FB Fielding.
Scorer: Jessop.

13/01/1894 v WARMLEY (H) Lost 0-3   Att: 400
SJF Kent; JL Somerville, HO Fowler; Walter Sessions, HH Scott, FM Stout; PW Stout, FB Fielding,
AC Cragg, HT Robins, HG Sherwood.

20/01/1894 v TROWBRIDGE TOWN (A) Lost 2-8
SJF Kent; AC Cragg, HO Fowler; FM Stout, HH Scott, T Clark; WG Matthews, HT Robins,
AF Fielding, HG Sherwood, FB Fielding.
Scorer: FB Fielding (2).

10/02/1894 v WARMLEY (A) Lost 0-2   Att: 600
SJF Kent; JL Somerville, CH Norrington; AC Cragg, HH Scott, FM Stout; WG Matthews, HT Robins,
HG Sherwood, AF Fielding, PM Stout.
(This line-up courtesy of The Gloucester Standard & Gloucestershire News)

17/02/1894 v MANGOTSFIELD (H) Won 4-2
SJF Kent; JL Somerville, AC Cragg; FM Stout, HH Scott, AC Hoitt; PW Stout, AF Fielding,
FB Fielding, WG Matthews, HT Robins.
Scorer: FB Fielding (4).

17/03/1894 v CLIFTON (A) Lost 2-6
(No match report in The Citizen).
Scorers: ?. (2 goals missing).

24/03/1894 v STAPLE HILL (A) Lost 1-3
HT Robins; JL Somerville, ETS Tadman; FM Stout, AC Hoitt, ? Ward; WG Matthews, ? Mason,
FB Fielding, PW Stout, HG Sherwood.
Scorer: ? (pen). (1 goal missing)

26/03/1894 v SAINT GEORGE (H) Lost 1-2
SJF Kent; JL Somerville, E Tadman; FM Stout, AC Hoitt, AC Cragg; FB Fielding, PW Stout,
JOT Powell, HG Sherwood, WG Matthews.
Scorer: Powell.

31/03/1894 v BEDMINSTER (H) Won 5-2   Att: Half-dozen!
SJF Kent; JL Somerville, AC Cragg; E Tadman, FM Stout, AC Hoitt; WG Matthews, HT Robins, HG Sherwood, FB Fielding, PW Stout.
Scorers: Matthews, PW Stout, FM Stout, FB Fielding, Somerville.
(Scorers courtesy of The Gloucester Standard & Gloucestershire News)

v CLEVEDON (A) Lost 0-1
missing

POS	CLUB	P	W	D	L	F	A	PTS
1	WARMLEY	18	12	5	1	32	13	27*
2	SAINT GEORGE	18	10	6	2	39	23	26
3	TROWBRIDGE TOWN	18	9	4	5	54	33	22
4	BEDMINSTER	18	9	2	7	41	36	20
5	CLEVEDON	18	7	5	6	34	40	19
6	CLIFTON	18	6	4	8	37	30	16
7	STAPLE HILL	18	5	5	8	23	33	15
8	GLOUCESTER	18	6	1	11	32	45	13
9	EASTVILLE ROVERS	18	5	2	11	30	39	12
10	MANGOTSFIELD	18	2	4	12	19	48	8
		180	71	38	71	341	340	178

* Two points deducted for misconduct.

Appearances: T Clark 2, AC Cragg 13, AF Fielding 3, FB Fielding 15, HO Fowler 2, RN Green 7, Rev.JH Harvey 7, AC Hoitt 4, A Jessop 1, AE Johnson 1, SJF Kent 15, ? Mason 1, WG Matthews 8, FM Morris 1, CH Norrington 1, ? Pennington, JOT Powell 1, HT Robins 15, HH Scott 13, Walter Sessions 2, Wilfred Sessions 1, HG Sherwood 14, JL Somerville 14, EF Stebbing 4, FM Stout 11, PW Stout 14, ETS Tadman 3, ? Ward 1.
Scorers: FB Fielding 8, PW Stout 8, HG Sherwood 3, WG Matthews 2, HT Robins 2, EF Stebbing 2, A Jessop 1, JOT Powell 1, JL Somerville 1, FM Stout 1 (Total 29).
Note: 2 line-ups missing and 3 goals missing.

1894-1895 – BRISTOL AND DISTRICT LEAGUE – FIRST DIVISION
(Gloucester played at Budding's Field)

06/10/1894 v CLIFTON (H) Won 4-3
G Speck; RC Fowler, CG Vaughan; AC Cragg, WT Pitt, FM Stout; AF Fielding, HG Sherwood, PW Stout, FB Fielding, ES Snell.
Scorers: Sherwood, PW Stout (2,1 pen), FB Fielding.

20/10/1894 v EASTVILLE ROVERS (H) Lost 1-2
G Speck; CG Vaughan, ETS Tadman; FM Stout, WT Pitt, AC Cragg; FB Fielding, EL Turner, PW Stout, HG Sherwood, AF Fielding.
Scorer: Sherwood.

27/10/1894 v CLIFTON (A) Lost 3-4
G Speck; AE Goodwin, ETS Tadman; AC Cragg, WT Pitt, FM Stout; FB Fielding, HG Sherwood, PW Stout, HT Robins, AF Fielding.
Scorers: PW Stout (2), FB Fielding.

03/11/1894 v CLEVEDON (H) Won 10-0
G Speck; AE Goodwin, ETS Tadman; WT Pitt, Rev. M Wade-Smith, AC Cragg; FB Fielding,
AF Fielding, PW Stout, WG Matthews, HT Robins.
Scorers: PW Stout (5), AF Fielding (3), FB Fielding (2).

17/11/1894 v SAINT GEORGE (H) Lost 1-2
G Speck; RC Fowler, ETS Tadman; FM Stout, Rev. M Wade-Smith, AC Cragg; AF Fielding,
FB Fielding, PW Stout, W "Bedman", HG Sherwood.
Scorer: Sherwood.

24/11/1894 v MANGOTSFIELD (A) Drew 1-1
G Speck; ? Burt, ETS Tadman; FM Stout, Rev. M Wade-Smith, JM Parker; AF Fielding, FB Fielding,
PW Stout, AC Cragg, HG Sherwood.
Scorer: PW Stout.

01/12/1894 v TROWBRIDGE TOWN (H) Lost 2-3
G Speck; ETS Tadman, ? Mansfield; JM Parker, Rev. M Wade-Smith, FM Stout; AF Fielding,
HT Robins, FB Fielding, HG Sherwood, AC Cragg.
Scorers: FB Fielding, Sherwood.

08/12/1894 v SWINDON WANDERERS (H) Won 2-0
G Speck; ETS Tadman, AC Cragg; JM Parker, Rev. M Wade-Smith, FM Stout; HG Sherwood,
ES Snell, PW Stout, AF Fielding, FB Fielding.
Scorers: Snell, PW Stout.

15/12/1894 v STAPLE HILL (A) Lost 0-2
(Only PW Stout mentioned in The Citizen and the others in The Gloucestershire Chronicle)
RC Fowler, AC Cragg, HT Robins, PW Stout.

22/12/1894 v HEREFORD THISTLE (A) Drew 6-6
G Speck; RC Fowler, AE Goodwin; FM.Morris, FM Stout, AC Cragg; AF Fielding, HT Robins,
FB Fielding, HG Sherwood, GC Clutterbuck.
Scorers: Sherwood (3), AF Fielding, FB Fielding, Cragg.

02/03/1895 v BEDMINSTER (H) Won 3-0
G Speck; ETS Tadman, CG Vaughan; FM Stout, Rev. M Wade-Smith, AC Cragg; FB Fielding,
AF Fielding, PW Stout, HG Sherwood, GC Clutterbuck.
Scorers: FB Fielding, ?. (2 goals missing).

09/03/1895 v SAINT GEORGE (A) Lost 1-3
G Speck; AE Goodwin, ETS Tadman; AC Cragg, Rev. M Wade-Smith, FM Stout; WG Matthews,
GC Clutterbuck, HG Sherwood, AF Fielding, FB Fielding.
Scorer: ?. (1 goal missing).

16/03/1895 v EASTVILLE ROVERS (A) Won 5-3
(Only six players mentioned in The Citizen) G Speck, AE Goodwin, M Wade-Smith, PW Stout,
HG Sherwood, FB Fielding.
Scorers: FB Fielding, PW Stout (4).

23/03/1895 v WARMLEY (H) Won 3-2
G Speck; RC Fowler, ETS Tadman; FM Stout, Rev. M Wade-Smith, AC Cragg; HG Sherwood, FM Morris, PW Stout, AF Fielding, FB Fielding.
Scorers: AF Fielding, Morris, FB Fielding.

25/03/1895 v STAPLE HILL (H) Drew 2-2
G Speck; RC Fowler, LH Carter; AC Cragg, Rev. M Wade-Smith, FM Morris; FM Stout, HG Sherwood, PW Stout, AF Fielding, FB Fielding.
Scorers: AF Fielding, ?. (1 goal missing).

30/03/1895 v CLEVEDON (A) Won 5-2
G Speck; RC Fowler, ETS Tadman; FM Morris, AC Cragg, Rev. M Wade-Smith; AF Fielding, C Pettey, FB Fielding, J Radford, HG Sherwood.
Scorers: ?. (5 goals missing).

06/04/1895 v BEDMINSTER (A) Won 5-3
(Only three players mentioned in The Citizen) FB Fielding, PW Stout, HG Sherwood.
Scorers: Sherwood, FB Fielding, PW Stout (3).

08/04/1895 v WARMLEY (A) Lost 0-7
(Only one player mentioned in The Citizen) HT Robins.

20/04/1895 v TROWBRIDGE TOWN (A) Won 4-0
G Speck; RC Fowler, H Barnard; FM Stout, Rev. M Wade-Smith, WT Pitt; AF Fielding, AP Frith, FB Fielding, J Radford, HT Robins.
Scorers: FB Fielding (2), Robins (2).

v HEREFORD THISTLE (H) missing

v MANGOTSFIELD (H) missing

v SWINDON WANDERERS (A) missing

POS	CLUB	P	W	D	L	F	A	PTS
1	HEREFORD THISTLE	22	18	3	1	93	21	39
2	SAINT GEORGE	22	18	3	1	76	21	39
3	WARMLEY	22	14	2	6	74	30	30
4	STAPLE HILL	22	11	4	7	56	38	26
5	GLOUCESTER	22	10	4	8	64	54	24
6	EASTVILLE ROVERS	22	10	4	8	46	40	24
7	TROWBRIDGE TOWN	22	9	4	9	68	48	22
8	CLIFTON	22	8	2	12	47	55	18
9	BEDMINSTER	22	7	0	15	39	73	14
10	SWINDON WANDERERS	22	5	3	14	40	63	13
11	MANGOTSFIELD	22	5	2	15	22	68	12
12	CLEVEDON	22	1	1	20	23	136	3
		264	116	32	116	648	647	264

Appearances: H Barnard 1, W "Bedman" 1, ? Burt 1, LH Carter 1, GC Clutterbuck 3, AC Cragg 15, AF Fielding 15, FB Fielding 17, RC Fowler 8, AP Frith 1, AE Goodwin 5, ? Mansfield 1, WG Matthews 2, FM Morris 4, JM Parker 3, C Pettey 1, WT Pitt 5, J Radford 2, HT Robins 7, HG Sherwood 15, ES Snell 2, G Speck 16, FM Stout 13, PW Stout 13, ETS Tadman 11, EL Turner 1, CG Vaughan 3, Rev. M Wade-Smith 12.
Scorers: PW Stout 18, FB Fielding 12, HG Sherwood 8, AF Fielding 6, HT Robins 2, AC Cragg 1, FM Morris 1, ES Snell 1 (Total 49).
Note: 3 line-ups missing, 4 partial line-ups and 15 goals missing. The Citizen for January and February 1895 missing at Gloucester Record Office.

1895-1896 – WESTERN LEAGUE – FIRST DIVISION
(Gloucester played at Avenue Road Ground (Tuffley Avenue))

28/09/1895 v SAINT PAUL'S (H) Drew 3-3
G Speck; AE Goodwin, RC Fowler; HH Scott, Rev. M Wade-Smith, A Spence; FB Fielding, AF Fielding, HD Green, HG Sherwood, GC Clutterbuck.
Scorers: Green (2), Sherwood.

05/10/1895 v TROWBRIDGE TOWN (A) Lost 1-3
HT Robins; AE Goodwin, RC Fowler; HH Scott, Rev. M Wade-Smith, A Spence; FB Fielding, AF Fielding, HD Green, J Radford, GC Clutterbuck.
Scorer: FB Fielding.

19/10/1895 v TROWBRIDGE TOWN (H) Lost 1-8
G Speck; AE Goodwin, HD Green; HH Scott, Rev. M Wade-Smith, A Spence; AF Fielding, FB Fielding, H Harris, HG Sherwood, GC Clutterbuck.
Scorer: FB Fielding.

26/10/1895 v SAINT GEORGE (H) Won 2-0
G Speck; AC Cragg, ETS Tadman; HH Scott, Rev. M Wade-Smith, GC Clutterbuck; AF Fielding, FB Fielding, H Harris, HG Sherwood, J Franklin.
Scorers: FB Fielding, Harris.

02/11/1895 v STAPLE HILL (A) Lost 1-3
G Speck; AC Cragg, ETS Tadman; HH Scott, Rev. M Wade-Smith, WT Pitt; AF Fielding, FB Fielding, GC Clutterbuck, C Pettey, AN Other.
Scorer: FB Fielding.

09/11/1895 v EASTVILLE ROVERS (A) Won 2-1
G Speck; ETS Tadman, AC Cragg; A Spence, HH Scott, Rev. M Wade-Smith; AF Fielding, FB Fielding, H Harris, AP Frith, HT Robins.
Scorers: FB Fielding, own goal.

30/11/1895 v CLIFTON (A) Won 6-2
G Speck; AC Cragg, ETS Tadman; A Spence, HH Scott, Rev. M Wade-Smith; AF Fielding, FB Fielding, ES Snell, GC Clutterbuck, AN Other.
Scorers: FB Fielding, Clutterbuck, ?. (4 goals missing).

07/12/1895 v WARMLEY (A) Lost 1-2
G Speck; AP Frith, ETS Tadman; A Spence, HH Scott, F Carely; AF Fielding, FB Fielding, H Harris, HT Robins, AN Other.
Scorer: FB Fielding.

14/12/1895 v MANGOTSFIELD (H) Won 4-0
G Speck; ETS Tadman, AP Frith; HH Scott, Rev. M Wade-Smith, A Spence; FB Fielding,
AF Fielding, HG Sherwood, AC Cragg, GC Clutterbuck.
Scorers: Clutterbuck (2), Sherwood, FB Fielding.

21/12/1895 v BEDMINSTER (A) Drew 0-0
G Speck; ETS Tadman, AP Frith; RC Fowler, HH Scott, A Spence; AF Fielding, FB Fielding,
HG Sherwood, AC Cragg, GC Clutterbuck.

04/01/1896 v SAINT PAUL'S (A) ?
G Speck; AP Frith, AC Cragg; A Spence, HH Scott, FM Morris; AF Fielding, FB Fielding,
HG Sherwood, F Pearce, AN Other.

18/01/1896 v CLIFTON (H) Lost 1-2
G Speck; ETS Tadman, AP Frith; A Spence, HH Scott, CF White; AF Fielding, E James, FB Fielding,
GC Clutterbuck, J Franklin.
Scorer; FB Fielding.

01/02/1896 v EASTVILLE ROVERS (H) Lost 2-3
G Speck; AP Frith, RC Fowler; A Spence, HH Scott, GC Clutterbuck; AF Fielding, FB Fielding,
H Harris, AC Cragg, HG Sherwood.
Scorer: FB Fielding (2).

08/02/1896 v STAPLE HILL (H) Lost 0-2
G Speck; ETS Tadman, AP Frith; RC Fowler, A Spence, WH Hicks; AF Fielding, FB Fielding,
HG Sherwood, AC Cragg, E James.

15/02/1896 v SAINT GEORGE (A) Lost 0-5
G Speck; AP Frith, ETS Tadman; A Spence, ? Mackay, WH Hicks; AF Fielding, FB Fielding,
GL Jessop, E James, AN Other.
(Score courtesy of Gloucester Standard & Gloucestershire News)

22/02/1896 v SWINDON WANDERERS (A) Lost 2-3
(Only one player mentioned in The Citizen) C Pettey.
Scorers: own goal, Pettey.

07/03/1896 v MANGOTSFIELD (A) Won 1-0
(Only two players mentioned in The Citizen and Sherwood in The Gloucestershire Chronicle. Only 10
men played of which three were debutants) G Speck; AF Fielding, HG Sherwood.
Scorer: Sherwood.

14/03/1896 v WARMLEY (H) Lost 1-4
G Speck; ETS Tadman, AP Frith; WT Pitt, WH Hicks, JA Oakey; H Daniells, AF Fielding,
FB Fielding, GL Jessop, HT Porter.
Scorer: Daniells.

00/04/1896 v BEDMINSTER (H) Draw
(Unplayed match. It was resolved that the game should be considered a draw and each club given one
point)

25/04/1896 v SWINDON WANDERERS (H) Draw
(Unplayed match. It was resolved that the game should be considered a draw and each club given one point)

POS	CLUB	P	W	D	L	F	A	PTS
1	WARMLEY	20	16	3	1	65	13	35
2	EASTVILLE ROVERS	20	14	1	5	57	22	29
3	STAPLE HILL	20	13	3	4	48	19	29
4	TROWBRIDGE TOWN	20	13	1	6	50	31	27
5	SAINT GEORGE	20	10	4	6	47	38	24
6	CLIFTON	20	8	3	9	44	50	17*
7	GLOUCESTER +	20	6	4	10	29	42	16
8	BEDMINSTER	20	6	2	12	36	41	14
9	SWINDON WANDERERS	20	4	4	12	22	57	12
10	MANGOTSFIELD	20	3	3	14	17	54	9
11	SAINT PAUL'S	20	2	2	16	12	60	6
12	CARDIFF							
		220	95	30	95	427	427	218

*Two points deducted for misconduct.
+ Gloucester v Bedminster and Gloucester v Swindon Wanderers unplayed. It was resolved that the games should be considered drawn and each club given one point. Cardiff withdrew. All scores were expunged from records.

Appearances: F Carely 1, GC Clutterbuck 10, AC Cragg 9, H Daniells 1, AF Fielding 17, FB Fielding 16, RC Fowler 5, J Franklin 2, AP Frith 10, AE Goodwin 3, HD Green 3, H Harris 5, WH Hicks 3, E James 3, GL Jessop 2, ? Mackay 1, FM Morris 1, JA Oakey 1, F Pearce 1, C Pettey 2, WT Pitt 2, HT Porter 1, J Radford 1, HT Robins 3, HH Scott 13, HG Sherwood 9, ES Snell 1, G Speck 16, A Spence 13, ETS Tadman 11, Rev. M Wade-Smith 8, CF White 1, AN Other 5.
Scorers: FB Fielding 11, GC Clutterbuck 3, HG Sherwood 3, HD Green 2, H Daniells 1, H Harris 1, C Pettey 1, own goals 2 (Total 24).
Note: 2 partial line-ups and 5 goals missing.

1896-1897

GLOUCESTER HAD WITHDRAWN FROM THE WESTERN LEAGUE AT THE END OF THE PREVIOUS SEASON DUE TO FINANCIAL PROBLEMS. GLOUCESTER STILL CONTINUED PLAYING DESPITE THE PROBLEMS. THEY PLAYED 16 FRIENDLY GAMES AND FOR THIS SEASON ONLY THEY SHARED WITH THE POST OFFICE CLUB THE CO-OPERATIVE FIELD, INDIA ROAD. GLOUCESTER PARTICIPATED IN THE NEWLY CONSTITUTED GLOUCESTER AND DISTRICT LEAGUE BECOMING ONE OF ITS FOUNDER MEMBERS. IN MANY MATCH REPORTS IN THE CITIZEN SUBSEQUENT TO THIS SEASON THEY REFERRED TO THE GLOUCESTER FOOTBALL TEAM AS 'THE CITIZENS.'

1897-1898 – GLOUCESTER AND DISTRICT LEAGUE – FIRST DIVISION
(Gloucester played at Budding's Field)

25/09/1897 v ROSS KYRLE (A) Won 3-0
(Only two players mentioned in The Citizen) HW Arkell, AJ Stephens.
Scorers: Arkell (2), Stephens.

02/10/1897 v TEWKESBURY ABBEY (A) Lost 0-2
(Only one player mentioned in The Tewkesbury Register) G Speck.

13/11/1897 v CAVENDISH HOUSE (A) Won 1-0
(Only one player mentioned in The Citizen) HT Porter.
Scorer: Porter.

20/11/1897 v PRICE WALKERS (A) Won 1-0
(Lane mentioned in The Citizen and Speck In The Gloucestershire Chronicle) G Speck; LA Lane.
Scorer: Lane.

27/11/1897 v ROSS TOWN (H) Won 4-1
G Speck; WH Hicks, SS Harris; WA Brown, AF Fielding, JA Oakey; FB Fielding, HG Sherwood, HT Porter, AJ Stephens, LA Lane.
Scorers: Sherwood, Porter (2), FB Fielding.

04/12/1897 v TEWKESBURY ABBEY (H) Won 5-0
(Only three players mentioned in The Citizen and Speck in The Tewkesbury Gazette) G Speck; AF Fielding, HG Sherwood, HT Porter.
Scorers: AF Fielding, Sherwood (3), Porter.

15/01/1898 v ROSS TOWN (A) Won 4-2
(Only these two players mentioned in The Citizen) HT Porter, FB Fielding.
Scorers: Porter (3), FB Fielding.

22/01/1898 v CAVENDISH HOUSE (H) Won 2-1
G Speck; WH Hicks, SS Harris; WA Brown, JA Oakey, JG Washbourn; LA Lane, G Saunders, HT Porter, HW Arkell, WT Gardner.
Scorers: Saunders, Porter.

04/02/1898 v PRICE WALKERS (H) Won 8-0
G Speck; WH Hicks, SS Harris; WA Brown, AF Fielding, JA Oakey; FB Fielding, HW Arkell, HG Sherwood, HT Porter, C Pettey.
Scorers: AF Fielding (2), Porter (2), FB Fielding (3), Oakey.

09/04/1898 v ROSS KYRLE (H) Drew 1-1
(Only one player mentioned in The Citizen) HG Sherwood.
Scorer: Sherwood.

POS	CLUB	P	W	D	L	F	A	PTS
1	GLOUCESTER	10	8	1	1	33	7	17
2	ROSS TOWN	10	7	0	3	24	10	14
3	ROSS KYRLE	10	5	1	4	19	22	11
4	PRICE WALKERS	10	3	1	6	9	23	7
5	TEWKESBURY ABBEY	10	3	0	7	10	18	6
6	CAVENDISH HOUSE (Cheltenham)	10	2	1	7	10	26	5
		60	28	4	28	105	106	60

Appearances: HW Arkell 4, WA Brown 3, AF Fielding 3, FB Fielding 3, WT Gardner 1, SS Harris 3, WH Hicks 3, LA Lane 2, JA Oakey 3, C Pettey 1, HT Porter 6, G Saunders 1, HG Sherwood 4, G Speck 6, AJ Stephens 2, JG Washbourn 1.

Scorers: HT Porter 10, FB Fielding 5, HG Sherwood 5, AF Fielding 3, HW Arkell 2, LA Lane 1, JA Oakey 1, G Saunders 1, AJ Stephens 1 (Total 29).
Note: 7 partial line-ups and 4 goals missing.

Champions Gloucester and District League 1897-8
Left to Right (Standing): W. L. BADHAM, S. HARRIS, G. SPECK, J. G. WASHBOURN
(Sitting): H. PORTER, J. A. OAKEY, W. H. HICKS (*Captain*), A. F. FIELDING, F. B. FIELDING
(Front): A. L. LANE, H. G. SHERWOOD, H. W. ARKELL

1898-1899 – GLOUCESTER AND DISTRICT LEAGUE – FIRST DIVISION
(Gloucester played at Avenue Road Ground (Tuffley Avenue))

08/10/1898 v LEDBURY VICTORIA (H) Won 6-0
G Speck; SS Harris, WH Hicks; B Guy, AF Fielding, H Lane; HT Porter, BH Lane, LA Lane, HG Sherwood, HW Arkell.
Scorers: LA Lane (3), Guy, AF Fielding, Porter.

22/10/1898 v EBLEY (H) Won 2-0
G Speck; HW Arkell, SS Harris; H Lane, AF Fielding, JA Oakey; FB Fielding, HG Sherwood, LA Lane, BH Lane, HT Porter.
Scorers: AF Fielding, Arkell.

29/10/1898 v TEWKESBURY ABBEY (A) Drew 1-1
G Speck; WH Hicks, SS Harris; JA Oakey, AF Fielding, H Lane; HW Arkell, HG Sherwood, LA Lane, BH Lane, HT Porter.
Scorer: Porter.

12/11/1898 v ROSS TOWN (A) Lost 1-2
(Only one player mentioned in The Gloucestershire Chronicle) HW Arkell.
Scorer: HW Arkell.

10/12/1898 v TEWKESBURY ABBEY (H) Won 7-1
(Only six players mentioned in The Tewkesbury Register) G Speck; AF Fielding, HW Arkell, HG Sherwood, LA Lane, HT Porter.
Scorers: Porter, Sherwood (3), AF Fielding, Arkell, LA Lane.

17/12/1898 v CHELTENHAM TOWN (H) Drew 1-1
(The Citizen missing at The Record Office)
Scorer: ?. (1 goal missing).

07/01/1899 v ROSS TOWN (H) Drew 1-1
G Speck; HW Arkell, SS Harris; JA Oakey, AF Fielding, H Lane; BH Lane, HG Sherwood, LA Lane, HT Porter, W Long.
Scorer: Sherwood.

28/01/1899 v LEDBURY VICTORIA (A) Drew 0-0
(No mention of Gloucester players in The Citizen).

18/02/1899 v EBLEY (A) Won 5-0
G Speck; HW Arkell, SS Harris; RR Sly, JA Oakey, H Lane; FT Rust, AF Fielding, AL Lane, HG Sherwood, HT Porter.
Scorers: Sherwood (2), own goal, Rust, Porter.

25/02/1899 v ROSS KYRLE (H) Lost 1-3
G Speck; HW Arkell, SS Harris; RR Sly, JA Oakey, H Lane; FT Rust, AF Fielding, LA Lane, HG Sherwood, HT Porter.
Scorer: AF Fielding.

18/03/1899 v ROSS KYRLE (A) Won 3-0
G Speck; HW Arkell, SS Harris; RR Sly, JA Oakey, H Lane; AF Fielding, FT Rust, LA Lane, HG Sherwood, HT Porter.
Scorers: own goals (2), Rust.

01/04/1899 v CHELTENHAM TOWN (A) Won 2-0
(Only seven players mentioned in The Citizen) G Speck; RR Sly, AF Fielding, HG Sherwood, FT Rust, W Long, HT Porter.
Scorers: Porter, Rust.

POS	CLUB	P	W	D	L	F	A	PTS
1	ROSS KYRLE	12	10	0	2	32	13	20
2	GLOUCESTER	12	6	4	2	30	9	16
3	ROSS TOWN	12	5	2	5	23	19	12
4	LEDBURY VICTORIA	12	4	3	5	14	19	11
5	TEWKESBURY ABBEY	12	3	3	6	12	28	9
6	EBLEY	12	3	2	7	19	22	8
7	CHELTENHAM TOWN	12	2	4	6	13	33	8
		84	33	18	33	143	143	84

Appearances: HW Arkell 9, AF Fielding 9, FB Fielding 1, B Guy 1, SS Harris 7, WH Hicks 2, BH Lane 4, H Lane 7, LA Lane 8, W Long 2, JA Oakey 6, HT Porter 9, FT Rust 4, HG Sherwood 9, RR Sly 4, G Speck 9.

Scorers: HG Sherwood 6, HT Porter 5, AF Fielding 4, LA Lane 4, FT Rust 3, HW Arkell 3, B Guy 1, own goals 3 (Total 29).
Note: 3 line-ups missing, 2 partial line-ups and 1 goal missing. The Citizen for November and December 1898 missing at Gloucester Record Office.

1899-1900 – GLOUCESTER AND DISTRICT LEAGUE – FIRST DIVISION
(Gloucester played at Avenue Road Ground (Tuffley Avenue))

18/11/1899 v ROSS TOWN (A) Won 4-1
(Only six players mentioned in The Citizen and Rust in The Gloucestershire Echo) F Hallett; HW Arkell, AF Fielding, RR Sly, FT Rust, HT Porter, WJ Hart.
Scorers: Arkell, AF Fielding, Hart, Porter.

25/11/1899 v CHELTENHAM TOWN (H) Won 2-1
F Hallett; HW Arkell, F Pinnegar; RR Sly, AF Fielding, E Keys; JW Stock, FT Rust, HT Porter, W Llewellyn, W Long.
Scorers: Llewellyn, Porter.

02/12/1899 v TEWKESBURY ABBEY (H) Drew 2-2
F Hallett; HW Arkell, F Pinnegar; RR Sly, AF Fielding, E Keys; W Long, W Shaw, HT Porter, FT Rust, HG Sherwood.
Scorers: Sherwood, Porter.
(This line-up courtesy of The Gloucestershire Echo).

09/12/1899 v ROSS KYRLE (A) Won 2-1
F Hallett; HW Arkell, F Pinnegar; H Lane, E Keys, RR Sly; J Wakefield, W Shaw, AF Fielding, FT Rust, HT Porter.
Scorers: Lane, Shaw.
(This line-up courtesy of The Gloucestershire Echo).

30/12/1899 v LEDBURY VICTORIA (H) Unplayed
F Hallett; HW Arkell, F Pinnegar; E Keys, AF Fielding, RR Sly; HT Porter, FT Rust, JW Stock, W Shaw, W Long.
(The above team was selected for 30/12/1899)

20/01/1900 v ROSS KYRLE (H) Won 6-0
F Hallett; HW Arkell, F Pinnegar; RR Sly, AF Fielding, E Keys; JW Stock, FT Rust, ST Rich, W Shaw, HT Porter.
Scorers: Shaw (2), AF Fielding (pen), Porter, Keys, Rust.

24/02/1900 v CHELTENHAM TOWN (A) Drew 3-3
F Hallett; HW Arkell, F Pinnegar; RR Sly, RF Morley, E Keys; JW Stock, FT Rust, AF Fielding, W Shaw, HT Porter.
Scorers: Porter (2), Shaw.

03/03/1900 v ROSS TOWN (H, Kingsholm) Won 3-2
F Hallett; HW Arkell, F Pinnegar; H Nicholls, E Keys, RR Sly; JW Stock, FT Rust, WJ Hart, W Shaw, HT Porter.
Scorers: Rust, Porter, Shaw.

10/03/1900 v LEDBURY VICTORIA (A) Won 2-1
(Only two players mentioned in The Citizen) RR Sly, HT Porter.
Scorers: ?. (2 goals missing).

24/03/1900 v TEWKESBURY ABBEY (A) Won 2-0
(Sly and Porter mentioned in The Citizen and Shaw and Wakefield in The Tewkesbury Register)
RR Sly, W Shaw, J Wakefield, HT Porter.
Scorers: Shaw, Wakefield.

POS	CLUB	P	W	D	L	F	A	PTS
1	GLOUCESTER	9	7	2	0	26	11	16
2	TEWKESBURY ABBEY	9	3	3	3	8	12	9
3	LEDBURY VICTORIA +	6	4	1	1	11	7	7*
4	CHELTENHAM TOWN	8	1	5	2	16	13	7
5	ROSS TOWN	10	3	2	5	15	17	6*
6	ROSS KYRLE	10	1	1	8	13	30	3
		52	19	14	19	89	90	48

* Two points deducted for playing ineligible players.
+ Ledbury Victoria notified their resignation from the League after 6 matches. Results stayed. Although research has Ledbury Victoria playing Gloucester in March so maybe this was their 6th match!
Ross Kyrle v Tewkesbury Abbey not played although recorded as played.
Tewkesbury Abbey awarded 2 points.

Appearances: HW Arkell 7, AF Fielding 6, F Hallett 7, WJ Hart 2, E Keys 6, H Lane 1, W Llewellyn 1, W Long 2, RF Morley 1, H Nicholls 1, F Pinnegar 6, HT Porter 9, ST Rich 1, FT Rust 7, W Shaw 6, HG Sherwood 1, RR Sly 9, JW Stock 4, J Wakefield 2.
Scorers: HT Porter 7, W Shaw 6, AF Fielding 2, FT Rust 2, HW Arkell 1, WJ Hart 1, E Keys 1, H Lane 1, W Llewellyn 1, HG Sherwood 1, J Wakefield 1 (Total 24).
Note: 4 partial line-ups and 2 goals missing.

1900-1901 – GLOUCESTER AND DISTRICT LEAGUE – FIRST DIVISION
(Gloucester played at Avenue Road Ground (Tuffley Avenue))

27/10/1900 v CHELTENHAM TRAINING COLLEGE (A) Lost 1-3
W Willetts; HW Arkell, F Pinnegar; TE Axford, E Keys, AF Fielding; J Wakefield, W Shaw, W Mason, FT Rust, HT Porter.
Scorer: Porter.

03/11/1900 v TEWKESBURY ABBEY (A) Lost 1-4
(Only two players mentioned in The Citizen and Mason in The Tewkesbury Register) W Willetts; W Mason, HT Porter.
Scorer: Porter.

24/11/1900 v ROSS TOWN (H) Won 6-0
W Willetts; HW Arkell, GR Arnold; AF Fielding, TE Axford, FR Crawley; J Wakefield, W Mason, HT Porter, W Shaw, C Wilson.
Scorers: Shaw, Wakefield (2), Wilson, ?. (2 goals missing).

01/12/1900 v CHELTENHAM TOWN (A) Lost 0-1
W Willetts; HW Arkell, GR Arnold; AF Fielding, FR Crawley, TE Axford; W Mason, FT Rust,
J Wakefield, C Wilson, HT Porter.

08/12/1900 v ROSELEIGH (A) Lost 2-3
? Stafford; JG Washbourn, HW Arkell; A James, FR Crawley, TE Axford; W Mason, ? Smith,
J Wakefield, C Wilson, HT Porter.
Scorers: Porter, Wilson.

19/01/1901 v CHELTENHAM TOWN (H, Buddings Field) Lost 0-2
W Willetts; WH Lambe, H Lane; FR Crawley, AF Fielding, TE Axford; W Mason, W Shaw,
J Wakefield, HT Porter, C Wilson.

09/02/1901 v CHELTENHAM TRAINING COLLEGE (H) Won 1-0
W Willetts; AF Fielding, HW Arkell; FR Crawley, DE Griffiths, TE Axford; J Wakefield, W Mason,
W Shaw, HT Porter, C Wilson.
Scorer: Wakefield.
(Abandoned at half-time ground unfit. Score stands)

09/03/1901 v TEWKESBURY ABBEY (H) Lost 1-5
(Only one player mentioned in The Tewkesbury Register) W Mason.
Scorer: ?. (1 goal missing).

16/03/1901 v ROSS TOWN (A) Drew 0-0
(Only three players mentioned in The Citizen) W Willetts; HW Arkell, C Wilson.

23/03/1901 v ROSELEIGH (H) Won
Unplayed match. Roseleigh had withdrawn from League. Win accorded to Gloucester.

POS	CLUB	P	W	D	L	F	A	PTS
1	TEWKESBURY ABBEY *	10	8	2	0	23	5	18
2	CHELTENHAM TOWN *	10	6	2	2	20	7	14
3	CHELTENHAM TRAINING COLLEGE *+	10	6	1	3	18	9	13
4	GLOUCESTER *+	10	3	1	6	12	18	7
5	ROSS TOWN	10	2	1	7	9	32	5
6	ROSELEIGH	10	1	1	8	5	16	3
		60	26	8	26	87	87	60

* These Clubs had two points awarded as the result of Roseleigh's withdrawal from the Division. In this table the matches have been reckoned as played and won by four teams.
+ The return fixture between these Clubs was abandoned at half-time owing to the state of the ground. The Training College subsequently conceded Gloucester two points.

Appearances: HW Arkell 6, GR Arnold 2, TE Axford 6, FR Crawley 5, AF Fielding 5,
DE Griffiths 1, A James 1, E Keys 1, WH Lambe 1, H Lane 1, W Mason 8, F Pinnegar 1,
HT Porter 7, FT Rust 2, W Shaw 4, ? Smith 1, ? Stafford 1, J Wakefield 6, JG Washbourn 1,
W Willetts 7, C Wilson 6.
Scorers: HT Porter 3, J Wakefield 3, C Wilson 2, W Shaw 1 (Total 9).
Note: 3 partial line-ups and 3 goals missing. Match scheduled for 26 January 1901 postponed due to Queen Victoria's death.

1901-1902

IN 1902, 'CITY' WAS FIRST ADDED TO THE GLOUCESTER TITLE SO I CAN ONLY ASSUME THAT THE GLOUCESTER CLUB HAD DISBANDED IN 1901 PRESUMABLY IN FINANCIAL DIFFICULTIES AGAIN AND RE-APPLIED TO THE GLOUCESTER AND DISTRICT LEAGUE UNDER THEIR NEW TITLE.

1902-1903 – GLOUCESTER AND DISTRICT LEAGUE – FIRST DIVISION
(Gloucester City played at Budding's Field)

01/11/1902 v ROSS TOWN (H) Drew 1-1
W Willetts; HW Arkell, EF Davy; SO Else, CFB Eddowes, RR Sly; J Wakefield, A Parker, FT Rust, AF Fielding, FCJ Romans.
Scorer: Parker.

03/01/1903 v CHELTENHAM TOWN (H) Lost 1-3
W Willetts; EF Davy, HW Arkell; FR Crawley, CFB Eddowes, RR Sly; J Wakefield, A Parker, FT Rust, AF Fielding, AN Other.
Scorer: Parker.

07/02/1903 v CHELTENHAM TOWN (A) Lost 1-6
J Hawkins; A Parker, HW Arkell; FR Crawley, CFB Eddowes, RR Sly; GW Fowler, J Wakefield, FT Rust, AF Fielding, FCJ Romans.
Scorer: Parker.

21/02/1903 v BOURTON ROVERS (H) Drew 1-1
W Willetts; WH Dee, HW Arkell; FR Crawley, CFB Eddowes, RR Sly; GW Fowler, A Parker, FT Rust, DE Griffiths, HL Richardson.
Scorer: ?. (1 goal missing).

28/02/1903 v ROSS TOWN (A) Lost 1-2
W Willetts; WD Vinson, HW Arkell; FR Crawley, CFB Eddowes, RR Sly; HL Richardson, A Parker, FT Rust, AF Fielding. GW Fowler.
Scorer: Parker.

14/03/1903 v TEWKESBURY ABBEY (H) Won 3-1
W Willetts; WD Vinson, HW Arkell; FR Crawley, CFB Eddowes, RR Sly; GW Fowler, A Parker, FT Rust, AF Fielding, FCJ Romans.
Scorers: Rust, Sly, Parker.

21/03/1903 v BOURTON ROVERS (A) Drew 1-1
W Willetts; WD Vinson, HW Arkell; FR Crawley, L Peckover, RR Sly; HL Richardson, GW Fowler, FT Rust, SJ Fielding, FCJ Romans.
Scorer: Rust (pen).

28/03/1903 v TEWKESBURY ABBEY (A) Drew 1-1
(Only Rust mentioned in The Citizen and the others in The Tewkesbury Register) W Willetts; HW Arkell, FT Rust.
Scorer: Rust.

POS	CLUB	P	W	D	L	F	A	PTS
1	CHELTENHAM TOWN	8	7	1	0	24	5	15
2	TEWKESBURY ABBEY	8	4	2	2	14	9	10
3	GLOUCESTER CITY	8	1	4	3	10	16	6
4	ROSS TOWN	8	2	1	5	11	15	5
5	BOURTON ROVERS	8	1	2	5	8	22	4
		40	15	10	15	67	67	40

Appearances: HW Arkell 8, FR Crawley 6, EF Davy 2, WH Dee 1, CFB Eddowes 6, SO Else 1, AF Fielding 5, SJ Fielding 1, GW Fowler 5, DE Griffiths 1, J Hawkins 1, A Parker 6, L Peckover 1, HL Richardson 3, FCJ Romans 4, FT Rust 8, RR Sly 7, WD Vinson 3, J Wakefield 3, W Willetts 7, AN Other 1.
Scorers: A Parker 5, FT Rust 3, RR Sly 1 (Total 9).
Note: 1 partial line-up and 1 goal missing.

1903-1904 – GLOUCESTER AND DISTRICT LEAGUE – FIRST DIVISION
(Gloucester City played at Budding's Field)

24/10/1903 v MIDLAND & SOUTH WESTERN JUNCTION RAILWAY (A) Won 6-1
W Willetts; EF Davy, A Lamb; FR Crawley, CFB Eddowes, TH Rust; J Wakefield, GR Arnold, A Parker, FT Rust, AF Fielding.
Scorers: FT Rust (5), Arnold.

07/11/1903 v CHELTENHAM TOWN (H) Won 2-0
W Willetts; EF Davy, HW Arkell; FR Crawley, CFB Eddowes, TH Rust; AF Fielding, FT Rust, A Parker, GR Arnold, J Wakefield.
Scorer: FT Rust (2).

28/11/1903 v SAINT MICHAEL'S (H) Lost 3-4
W Willetts; EF Davy, HW Arkell; TH Rust, CFB Eddowes, FR Crawley; AF Fielding, FT Rust, A Parker, E Keys, J Wakefield.
Scorers: Parker, FT Rust, TH Rust.

23/01/1904 v CIRENCESTER TOWN (H) Won 4-1
C Murray; T Trueman, EF Davy; FR Crawley, CFB Eddowes, TH Rust; J Wakefield, E Keys, A Parker, FT Rust, AF Fielding.
Scorers: Fielding, Parker, FT Rust, own goal.

06/02/1904 v BOURTON ROVERS (H) Won 2-1
(Only two players mentioned in The Gloucestershire Echo) A Parker, ? Boonavalle.
Scorers: Parker, Boonavalle.

25/02/1904 v TEWKESBURY TOWN (A) Won 2-1
AS Hoare; EF Davy, CFB Eddowes; FR Crawley, TH Rust, RR Sly; J Wakefield, T Trueman, A Parker, FT Rust, AF Fielding.
Scorers: Wakefield, FT Rust.

27/02/1904 v CHELTENHAM TOWN (A) Won 5-1
(Only four players mentioned in The Citizen) T Trueman, FR Crawley, J Wakefield, FT Rust.
Scorers: Crawley, FT Rust (2), Trueman, Wakefield.

03/03/1904 v MIDLANDS & SOUTH WESTERN JUNCTION RAILWAY (H) Won 3-1
AS Hoare; CFB Eddowes, EF Davy; RR Sly, TH Rust, AN Other; HL Richardson, FT Rust, A Parker,
T Trueman, J Wakefield.
Scorers: FT Rust (2), Parker.

05/03/1904 v TEWKESBURY TOWN (H) Drew 1-1
W Jones; EF Davy, CFB Eddowes; RR Sly, TH Rust, FR Crawley; AF Fielding, FT Rust, A Parker,
T Trueman, J Wakefield.
Scorer: FT Rust (pen).

12/03/1904 v SAINT MICHAEL'S (A) Lost 0-1
W Jones; CFB Eddowes, EF Davy; RR Sly, TH Rust, FR Crawley; AF Fielding, FT Rust, A Parker,
HL Richardson, J Wakefield.

19/03/1904 v CIRENCESTER TOWN (A) Won 6-0
(No match report in The Citizen).
Scorers: ?. (6 goals missing).

24/03/1904 v BOURTON ROVERS (A) Won 3-0
(Only these four players mentioned in The Gloucestershire Echo) TH Rust, ? Lewis, A Parker,
J Wakefield.
Scorers: Lewis, Parker, Wakefield.

POS	CLUB	P	W	D	L	F	A	PTS
1	GLOUCESTER CITY	12	9	1	2	37	12	19
2	SAINT MICHAEL'S	11	7	2	2	24	15	16
3	TEWKESBURY TOWN	10	6	3	1	23	8	15
4	MIDLAND & SOUTH WESTERN JUNCTION RAILWAY	9	4	1	4	15	16	9
5	CHELTENHAM TOWN	11	3	0	8	12	24	6
6	CIRENCESTER TOWN	10	1	2	7	6	31	4
7	BOURTON ROVERS	9	1	1	7	6	17	1*
		72	31	10	31	123	123	70

* Two points deducted for playing an ineligible man.
The Citizen of 26 March 1904 would indicate this as possible Final Table as winners of cups and medals announced.

Appearances: HW Arkell 2, GR Arnold 2, ? Boonavalle 1, FR Crawley 8, EF Davy 8,
CFB Eddowes 8, AF Fielding 7, AS Hoare 2, W Jones 2, E Keys 2, A Lamb 1, ? Lewis 1,
C Murray 1, A Parker 10, HL Richardson 2, FT Rust 9, TH Rust 9, RR Sly 4, T Trueman 5,
J Wakefield 10, W Willetts 3, AN Other 1.
Scorers: FT Rust 15, A Parker 5, J Wakefield 3, GR Arnold 1, ? Boonavalle 1, FR Crawley 1,
AF Fielding 1, ? Lewis 1, TH Rust 1, T Trueman 1, own goal 1 (Total 31).
Note: 2 line-ups missing, 2 partial line-ups and 6 goals missing.

1904-1905, 1905-1906

GLOUCESTER CITY WAS DISBANDED AGAIN IN 1904. IN 1906 GLOUCESTER CITY AMALGAMATED WITH THE HEMPSTED CLUB OF SAINT MICHAEL'S. IT WAS RECOGNISED THAT A CITY COMBINATION WOULD OFFER GREATER POSSIBILITIES FOR THE ADVANCEMENT OF SOCCER IN GLOUCESTER AND THE DISTRICT. THE 'NEW' CLUB APPLIED TO REJOIN THE GLOUCESTER AND DISTRICT LEAGUE STAYING FOR ONE SEASON BEFORE JOINING THE INAUGURAL NORTH GLOUCESTERSHIRE LEAGUE IN 1907.

1906-1907 –GLOUCESTER AND DISTRICT LEAGUE – FIRST DIVISION
(Gloucester City played at Budding's Field)

03/11/1906 v TEWKESBURY TOWN (H) Won 6-1
W Willetts; FE Taylor, FE Quixley; GA Vinson, AV Boughton, AH Smith; FEA Crouch, CH Haddon, N Squier, AE Kent, W Smith.
Scorers: Haddon, Boughton, Squier (2), Kent, Crouch.

24/11/1906 v SAINT PAUL'S UNITED (A) Lost 1-3
W Willetts; FW Dee, FE Quixley; GA Vinson, AV Boughton, AH Smith; WD Niblett, H Smith, N Squier, CH Haddon, JM Baldwin.
Scorer: ?. (1 goal missing).

08/12/1906 v CHELTENHAM TOWN (H) Won 6-1
W Willetts; FE Taylor, FE Quixley; GA Vinson, AV Boughton, AH Smith; CH Haddon, H Smith, N Squier, A Carter, JM Baldwin.
Scorers: Squier, H Smith (2), Baldwin (2), Haddon.

23/02/1907 v CHELTENHAM TOWN (A) Won 4-1
W Willetts; EF Davy, FE Quixley; GA Vinson, AV Boughton, AH Smith; CH Haddon, H Smith, N Squier, JM Baldwin, W Smith.
Scorers: Squier (2), Baldwin (2).

02/03/1907 v TEWKESBURY TOWN (A) Won 2-1
W Willetts; EF Davy, FE Quixley; GA Vinson, AV Boughton, AH Smith; CH Haddon, H Smith, N Squier, JM Baldwin, W Smith.
Scorer: Squier (2).

09/03/1907 v SAINT PAUL'S UNITED (H) Lost 0-1
W Willetts; EF Davy, FE Quixley; GA Vinson, AH Smith, AE Kent; CH Haddon, H Smith, N Squier, JM Baldwin, W Smith.

POS	CLUB	P	W	D	L	F	A	PTS
1	SAINT PAUL'S UNITED	6	3	3	0	10	5	9
2	GLOUCESTER CITY	6	4	0	2	19	8	8
3	CHELTENHAM TOWN	6	1	2	3	7	18	4
4	TEWKESBURY TOWN	6	1	1	4	8	13	3
5	BOURTON ROVERS							
		24	9	6	9	44	44	24

Bourton Rovers withdrew during season. All records expunged
One score is missing Saint Paul's United v Cheltenham Town although it is known

to have ended in a draw as it was reported Gloucester City missed out on the Championship by one point.

Appearances: JM Baldwin 5, AV Boughton 5, AJ Carter 1, FEA Crouch 1, EF Davy 3, FW Dee 1, CH Haddon 6, AE Kent 2, WD Niblett 1, FE Quixley 6, AH Smith 6, H Smith 5,W Smith 4, N Squier 6, FE Taylor 2, GA Vinson 6, W Willetts 6.
Scorers: N Squier 7, JM Baldwin 4, CH Haddon 2, H Smith 2, AV Boughton 1, FEA Crouch 1,AE Kent 1(Total 18).
Note: 1 goal missing.

1907-1908 – NORTH GLOUCESTERSHIRE LEAGUE – FIRST DIVISION
(Gloucester City played at Budding's Field)

12/10/1907 v SHARPNESS (A) Won 6-3
WT Blake; EF Davy, WD Vinson; GA Vinson, AV Boughton, J Hill; OJ Lucas, R Turner, N Squier, AJ Carter, AE Kent.
Scorers: Turner (3), Squier (2,1pen), Kent.

26/10/1907 v STROUD (A) Won 10-1
WT Blake; EF Davy, FE Quixley; GA Vinson, AV Boughton, AH Smith; OJ Lucas, R Turner, N Squier, AJ Carter, AE Kent.
Scorers: Carter (3,1pen), Lucas (2), Turner (4), Vinson.

02/11/1907 v TEWKESBURY TOWN (H) Won 4-0
WT Blake; EF Davy, FE Quixley; GA Vinson, AV Boughton, AH Smith; OJ Lucas, R Turner, N Squier, AJ Carter, AE Kent.
Scorers: Squier (2), Carter (2).

23/11/1907 v STROUD (H) Won 10-0
WT Blake; EF Davy, FE Quixley; GA Vinson, AV Boughton, AH Smith; OJ Lucas, R Turner,
N Squier, AJ Carter, AE Kent.
Scorers: Turner (5), Squier (4), Carter.

30/11/1907 v LINDEN OLD BOYS (H) Won 10-1
WT Blake; EF Davy, FE Quixley; GA Vinson, AV Boughton, AH Smith; OJ Lucas, AJ Carter,
N Squier, R Turner, AE Kent.
Scorers: Carter, Squier (4), Turner (5).

25/01/1908 v MIDLANDS & SOUTH WESTERN JUNCTION RAILWAY (H) Lost 1-2
WC Vickery; EF Davy, FE Quixley; GA Vinson, AV Boughton, AH Smith; AE Kent, AJ Carter,
N Squier, CH Haddon, F Bottomley.
Scorer: ?. (1 goal missing).

15/02/1908 v TEWKESBURY TOWN (A) Drew 1-1
WC Vickery; EF Davy, FE Quixley; GA Vinson, AH Smith, J Hill; AE Kent, OJ Lucas, N Squier,
AJ Carter, F Bottomley.
Scorer: Davy.

22/02/1908 v LINDEN OLD BOYS (A) Won 4-0
WC Vickery; EF Davy, FE Quixley; GA Vinson, AV Boughton, AH Smith; CH Haddon, OJ Lucas,
N Squier, AJ Carter, AE Kent.
Scorers: Kent (2), Smith, Squier.

29/02/1908 v SHARPNESS (H) Drew 1-1
WC Vickery; EF Davy, FE Quixley; GA Vinson, AV Boughton, AH Smith; CH Haddon, OJ Lucas,
N Squier, AJ Carter, AE Kent.
Scorer: Lucas.
(Goalscorer courtesy of The Dursley, Berkeley & Sharpness Gazette & Wotton-Under-Edge
Advertiser)

07/03/1908 v CHELTENHAM TOWN (A) Won 3-0
WC Vickery; EF Davy, FE Quixley; GA Vinson, AV Boughton, J Hill; HW Hale, AL Haydon,
AH Smith, AJ Carter, AE Kent.
Scorers: Hill, Carter (2).

14/03/1908 v SAINT PAUL'S UNITED (A) Won 3-1
WC Vickery; EF Davy, FE Quixley; GA Vinson, AV Boughton, AH Smith; N Squier, OJ Lucas,
HW Hale, AJ Carter, AE Kent.
Scorers: Squier (2), Smith.

18/03/1908 v CHELTENHAM TOWN (H) Won 2-1
WC Vickery; EF Davy, FE Quixley; GA Vinson, AV Boughton, AH Smith; CH Haddon, N Squier,
OJ Lucas, AJ Carter, AE Kent.
Scorers: Kent, Haddon.

28/03/1908 v MIDLANDS & SOUTH WESTERN JUNCTION RAILWAY (A) Won 4-1
WC Vickery; EF Davy, FE Quixley; GA Vinson, AV Boughton, AH Smith; CH Haddon, N Squier,
OJ Lucas, AJ Carter, AE Kent.
Scorers: Squier, Lucas, ?. (2 goals missing).

11/04/1908 v SAINT PAUL'S UNITED (H, Barnwood) Won 3-1
(Only seven players mentioned in The Citizen) WC Vickery; EF Davy, GA Vinson, AV Boughton, OJ Lucas, AJ Carter, AE Kent.
Scorers: Davy, Lucas, Carter.

POS	CLUB	P	W	D	L	F	A	PTS
1	GLOUCESTER CITY	14	12	1	1	61	13	25
2	STROUD	14	8	2	4	31	35	18
3	SHARPNESS	14	7	3	4	47	27	17
4	MIDLAND & SOUTH WESTERN JUNCTION RAILWAY	14	7	2	5	28	24	16
5	SAINT PAUL'S UNITED	14	4	4	6	24	23	12
6	TEWKESBURY TOWN	14	5	2	7	23	31	12
7	CHELTENHAM TOWN	14	3	2	9	11	30	8
8	LINDEN OLD BOYS	14	2	2	10	17	59	4
		112	48	18	46	242	242	112

Appearances: WT Blake 5, FE Bottomley 2, AV Boughton 13, AJ Carter 14, EF Davy 14, CH Haddon 5, HW Hale 2, AL Haydon 1, J Hill 3, AE Kent 14, OJ Lucas 12, FE Quixley 12, AH Smith 12, N Squier 12, R Turner 5, WC Vickery 9, GA Vinson 14, WD Vinson 1.
Scorers: R Turner 17, N Squier 16, AJ Carter 10, OJ Lucas 5, AE Kent 4, EF Davy 2, AH Smith 2, CH Haddon 1, J Hill 1, GAVinson 1 (Total 59).
Note: 1 partial line-up and 2 goals missing.

Winners of the North Gloucestershire League Cup and Medals—1st Division
Season 1907-8
Left to Right (Standing): F. E. TAYLOR (Committee), A. V. BOUGHTON, N. SQUIER, O. J. A. CARTER (Committee), W. C. VICKERY, F. E. QUIXLEY, C. M. WIGGIN (Assistant Hon. Secretary)
(Sitting): E. W. HUNT (Committee), W. G. REYNOLDS (Committee), C. H. HADDON, A. H. SMITH, E. F. DAVY (Captain), A. J. CARTER, G. A. VINSON, J. E. PALMER (Hon. Secretary), J. DAVY (Committee)
(Front): O. J. LUCAS, A. E. KENT

1908-1909 – NORTH GLOUCESTERSHIRE LEAGUE – FIRST DIVISION
(Gloucester City played at Budding's Field)

03/10/1908 v MIDLANDS & SOUTH WESTERN JUNCTION RAILWAY (H) Won 3-1
WC Vickery; FE Quixley, FE Taylor; GA Vinson, AV Boughton, AH Smith; CH Haddon, E Simpson, A Watts, AJ Carter, AE Kent.
Scorers: Kent, Watts (2).

14/11/1908 v STROUD (A) Drew 0-0
WC Vickery; WD Vinson, FE Quixley; GA Vinson, AH Smith, J Hill; E Simpson, A Watts, N Squier, AE Kent, W Smith.

21/11/1908 v MIDLANDS & SOUTH WESTERN JUNCTION RAILWAY (A) Drew 1-1
WC Vickery; WD Vinson, FE Quixley; GA Vinson, AH Smith, J Hill; AE Kent, A Watts, N Squier, AJ Carter, W Smith.
Scorer: Squier (pen).

05/12/1908 v SAINT PAUL'S UNITED (A) Won 4-3
WC Vickery; WD Vinson, RM Palmer; GA Vinson, AH Smith, J Hill; AE Kent, AJ Carter, WA Jarman, A Watts, W Smith.
Scorers: Jarman (3), ?. (1 goal missing).

12/12/1908 v STROUD (H) Won 2-0
WC Vickery; WD Vinson, FE Quixley; GA Vinson, AH Smith, J Hill; AE Kent, N Squier, A Watts, AJ Carter, W Smith.
Scorers: ?. (2 goals missing).

19/12/1908 v CHELTENHAM TOWN (H) Won 3-2
WC Vickery; FE Quixley, WD Vinson; GA Vinson, AH Smith, J Hill; AE Kent, A Watts, WA Jarman, AJ Carter, W Smith.
Scorers: Jarman (2), Carter.

02/01/1909 v DURSLEY (H) Won 6-0
WC Vickery; WD Vinson, FE Quixley; GA Vinson, AH Smith, J Hill; S Cook, AJ Carter, WA Jarman, L Butler, W Smith.
Scorers: Hill, Carter, Jarman (2), W Smith (2).

23/01/1909 v DURSLEY (A) Won 4-1
WC Vickery; WD Vinson, FE Quixley; GA Vinson, AH Smith, J Hill; E Simpson, A Watts, WA Jarman, AE Kent, W Smith.
Scorers: Watts (2,1pen), W Smith (2).
(One of Smith's goals courtesy of The Dursley, Berkeley & Sharpness Gazette & Wotton-Under-Edge Advertiser)

30/01/1909 v SAINT PAUL'S UNITED (H) Won 6-0
WC Vickery; WD Vinson, FE Quixley; GA Vinson, AH Smith, J Hill; N Squier, A Watts, WA Jarman, W Smith, AE Kent.
Scorers: W Smith (2), Kent, Jarman (2), Watts.

20/02/1909 v SHARPNESS (A) Drew 2-2
WC Vickery; WD Vinson, FE Quixley; GA Vinson, AH Smith, J Hill; AE Kent, W Smith, WA Jarman, A Watts, E Simpson.
Scorer: Jarman (2).

27/02/1909 v TEWKESBURY TOWN (H) Won 3-0
WC Vickery; WD Vinson, FE Quixley; GA Vinson, AH Smith, J Hill; E Simpson, A Watts, WA Jarman, W Smith, AE Kent.
Scorers: W Smith, Jarman, Watts.

13/03/1909 v TEWKESBURY TOWN (A) Won 3-0
WC Vickery; WD Vinson, FE Quixley; GA Vinson, AH Smith, J Hill; E Simpson, A Watts, WA Jarman, W Smith, AE Kent.
Scorers: W Smith, Simpson, Jarman.

17/03/1909 v SHARPNESS (H) Won 8-0
WC Vickery; WD Vinson, FE Quixley; GA Vinson, AH Smith, J Hill; E Simpson, A Watts, WA Jarman, N Squier, AE Kent.
Scorers: Simpson, Jarman (3), Squier (2), Watts, Kent.

20/03/1909 v CHELTENHAM TOWN (A) Won 3-0
WC Vickery; WD Vinson, FE Quixley; GA Vinson, AH Smith, J Hill; E Simpson, N Squier, WA Jarman, A Watts, AE Kent.
Scorers: own goal, Squier (2).

POS	CLUB	P	W	D	L	F	A	PTS
1	GLOUCESTER CITY	14	11	3	0	48	10	25
2	STROUD	12	7	3	2	37	21	17
3	SHARPNESS	12	6	5	1	43	31	17
4	TEWKESBURY TOWN	14	7	3	4	33	25	17
5	CHELTENHAM TOWN	14	3	4	7	25	33	10
6	DURSLEY	13	2	3	8	24	41	7
7	SAINT PAUL'S UNITED	14	3	1	10	22	45	7
8	MIDLAND & SOUTH WESTERN JUNCTION RAILWAY	13	2	2	9	22	52	6
		106	41	24	41	254	258	106

To early April 1909 only. Some fixtures missing. Could not find in The Citizen.

Appearances: AV Boughton 1, L Butler 1, AJ Carter 6, S Cook 1, CH Haddon 1, J Hill 13, WA Jarman 10, AE Kent 13, RM Palmer 1, FE Quixley 13, E Simpson 8, AH Smith 14, W Smith 11, N Squier 6, FE Taylor 1, WC Vickery 14, GA Vinson 14, WD Vinson 13, A Watts 13.
Scorers: WA Jarman 16, W Smith 8, A Watts 7, N Squier 5, AE Kent 3, AJ Carter 2, E Simpson 2, J Hill 1, own goal 1 (Total 45).
Note: 3 goals missing.

1909-1910 – NORTH GLOUCESTERSHIRE LEAGUE – FIRST DIVISION
(Gloucester City played at Budding's Field)

16/10/1909 v CHELTENHAM TOWN (H) Won 2-1
WC Vickery; W Ingles, JG Eldridge; GA Vinson, A Watts, J Hill; S Cook, L Bathurst, WA Jarman, W Smith, AE Kent.
Scorers: Jarman, Smith.

11/12/1909 v CHELTENHAM TOWN (A) Lost 1-2
WC Vickery; LA Carleton, W Ingles; GA Vinson, A Watts, J Hill; WA Jarman, ? Benbow, N Squier, W Smith, S Cook.
Scorer: own goal.

08/01/1910 v STROUD (H) Drew 2-2
WC Vickery; W Ingles, LA Carleton; GA Vinson, AH Smith, J Hill; C Barnes, JT Parsons, WA Jarman, W Smith, C Carter.
Scorers: W Smith, Jarman.

15/01/1910 v BRIMSCOMBE (A) Lost 0-3
WC Vickery; W Ingles; GA Vinson, AH Smith, J Hill; AE Kent, A Watts, WA Jarman, W Smith, JT Parsons (only ten players used).

22/01/1910 v TEWKESBURY TOWN (A) Won 4-2
WC Vickery; LA Carleton, W Ingles; GA Vinson, A Watts, CG Carter; S Cook, JT Parsons, WA Jarman, W Smith, AE Kent.
Scorers: Cook, own goal, Smith, Carter.

29/01/1910 v SHARPNESS (A) Lost 1-2
WC Vickery; W Ingles, LA Carleton; GA Vinson, FE Quixley, ? Williams; AE Kent, A Watts, WA Jarman, AH Smith, W Smith.
Scorer: Williams.

10/02/1910 v TEWKESBURY TOWN (H) Won 5-2
WC Vickery; LA Carleton, W Ingles; GA Vinson, A Watts, CG Carter; S Cook, C Durrett, WA Jarman, W Smith, AE Kent.
Scorers: Durrett (2), Ingles, Carter (pen), Kent.

12/02/1910 v STROUD (A) Lost 2-4
WC Vickery; LA Carleton, W Ingles; GA Vinson, A Watts, CG Carter; S Cook, AH Smith, WA Jarman, W Smith, AE Kent.
Scorers: W Smith, Carter.

03/03/1910 v SHARPNESS (H, Gloucester Old Boys Ground, Denmark Road) Drew 3-3
(Only four players mentioned in The Dursley, Berkeley & Sharpness Gazette & Wotton-Under-Edge Advertiser) GB Brace; S Cook, WA Jarman, AE Kent.
Scorers: Jarman, Cook (2).

05/03/1910 v SAINT PAUL'S UNITED (H) Won 5-1
WC Vickery: W Ingles, CG Carter; GA Vinson, AH Smith, J Hill; S Cook, A Watts, WA Jarman, W Smith, AE Kent.
Scorers: AH Smith, Jarman (2, 1pen), Cook, Ingles.

28/03/1910 v BRIMSCOMBE (H) Drew 1-1
GB Brace; W Ingles, ? Trueman; GA Vinson, AH Smith, CG Carter; HGH Davoll, AE Kent, A Watts, W Smith, JT Parsons.
Scorer: AH Smith.

23/04/1910 v SAINT PAUL'S UNITED (A) Drew 1-1
WC Vickery; W Ingles, LA Carleton; TT Vickery, FE Quixley, J Hill; CE Brown, FE Taylor, S Cook, JT Parsons, C Carter.
Scorer: Parsons.
(This result also counted for The Cheltenham & District League. Played 35 minutes each way).

POS	CLUB	P	W	D	L	F	A	PTS
1	SHARPNESS	12	8	3	1	45	13	19
2	BRIMSCOMBE	12	7	2	3	29	24	16
3	TEWKESBURY TOWN	12	6	1	5	28	28	13
4	GLOUCESTER CITY	12	4	4	4	26	24	10*
5	CHELTENHAM TOWN	12	3	3	6	16	19	9
6	SAINT PAUL'S UNITED	12	2	5	5	14	24	9
7	STROUD	12	2	2	8	20	46	6
		84	32	20	32	178	178	82

*Two points deducted for playing ineligible man v Sharpness and the goal scored by them disallowed.

Appearances: C Barnes 1, L Bathurst 1, ? Benbow 1, GB Brace 2, CE Brown 1, LA Carleton 7, C Carter 2, CG Carter 5, S Cook 8, HGH Davoll 1, C Durrett 1, JG Eldridge 1, J Hill 6, W Ingles 10, WA Jarman 10, AE Kent 9, JT Parsons 5, FE Quixley 2, AH Smith 6, W Smith 10, N Squier 1, FE Taylor, 1, ? Trueman 1, TT Vickery 1, WC Vickery 10, GA Vinson 10, A Watts 9, ? Williams 1.
Scorers: WA Jarman 5, S Cook 4, W Smith 4, CG Carter 3, C Durrett 2, W Ingles 2, AH Smith 2, AE Kent 1, JT Parsons 1, own goals 2 (Total 26).
Notes: 1 partial line-up missing.

1910-1911, 1911-1912, 1912-1913

GLOUCESTER CITY DISBANDED AGAIN. COINCIDENTALLY THE GLOUCESTER YMCA CLUB WAS FORMED IN 1910. INITIALLY THEY PARTICIPATED IN THE MINOR GLOUCESTER AND DISTRICT THURSDAY LEAGUE. GLOUCESTER YMCA DID ENTER A TEAM IN THE NORTH GLOUCESTERSHIRE LEAGUE IN 1913-1914.

1913-1914 – NORTH GLOUCESTERSHIRE LEAGUE – SECOND DIVISION
(Gloucester YMCA played at Llanthony, Hempsted)

04/10/1913 v MITCHELDEAN (H) Drew 1-1
HGH Davoll; JM McFarlane, CA Bretherton; F Corbett, JB Shadgett, FL Mills; ER Danks, HE Searles, EJ Jones, EE Allen, JT Parsons.
Scorer: ?. (1 goal missing).

18/10/1913 v WESTGATE (A) Lost 1-2
HGH Davoll; JM McFarlane, CA Bretherton; C Durrett, JB Shadgett, FL Mills; ER Danks, HE Searles, EJ Jones, LF Dudbridge, JT Parsons.
Scorer: ?. (1 goal missing).

01/11/1913 v LONGHOPE UNITED (H) Lost 0-3
HGH Davoll; JM McFarlane, CA Bretherton; P Bygrave, JB Shadgett, FL Mills; ER Danks, EE Allen, EJ Jones, LF Dudbridge, JT Parsons.

08/11/1913 v MINSTERWORTH (H) Lost 0-5
JH Rhodes; JM McFarlane, CA Bretherton; JB Shadgett, C Durrett, JB Lane; FL Mills, EE Allen, EJ Jones, LF Dudbridge, JT Parsons.

29/11/1913 v NEWNHAM EXCELSIOR (A) Lost 0-2
(No information in The Citizen).

20/12/1913 v TUFFLEY & WHADDON (A) Lost 0-4
(No information in The Citizen).

24/01/1914 v TUFFLEY & WHADDON (H) Lost 1-5
HGH Davoll; JM McFarlane, CA Bretherton; JB Lane, JB Shadgett, FL Mills; ER Danks, EE Allen,
EJ Jones, JT Parsons, LF Dudbridge.
Scorer: ?. (1 goal missing).

21/02/1914 v MINSTERWORTH (A) Lost 0-2
AN Other; JB Lane, CA Bretherton; JH Merrett, JB Shadgett, FL Mills; ER Danks, EE Allen, C Sides,
JT Parsons, LF Dudbridge.

07/03/1914 v LONGHOPE UNITED (A) ?
HGH Davoll; JM McFarlane, CA Bretherton; JB Shadgett, C Sides, JB Lane; ER Danks, EE Allen,
EJ Jones, AM Barrett, FL Mills.

14/03/1914 v WESTGATE (H) Won 4-0
(Only four players mentioned in The Citizen) HGH Davoll; JB Shadgett, ER Danks, EJ Jones.
Scorers: Danks, Shadgett, Jones, Davoll (pen).

28/03/1914 v NEWNHAM EXCELSIOR (H) Won 2-0
(No information in The Citizen).

18/04/1914 v MITCHELDEAN (N, Minsterworth) ?
(No information in The Citizen).

POS	CLUB	P	W	D	L	F	A	PTS
1	TUFFLEY & WHADDON	12	10	1	1	52	11	21
2	WESTGATE	12	6	3	3	35	18	15
3	LONGHOPE UNITED	12	4	5	3	31	23	13
4	MITCHELDEAN	11	4	4	3	18	12	12
5	MINSTERWORTH	12	2	5	5	18	20	9
6	NEWNHAM EXCELSIOR	12	2	3	7	18	57	7
7	GLOUCESTER YMCA	11	1	3	7	11	30	5
8	HATHERLEY UNITED							
		82	29	24	29	183	171	82

Hatherley United having applied to withdraw from the competition their record is eliminated.
Gloucester YMCA agreed to play Mitcheldean on 18 April 1914. Cannot find result in The Citizen.
Results and League Table do not add up.

Appearances: EE Allen 6, AM Barrett 1, CA Bretherton 7, P Bygrave 1, F Corbett 1,
ER Danks 7, HGH Davoll 6, LF Dudbridge 5, C Durrett 2, EJ Jones 7, JB Lane 4,
JM McFarlane 6, JH Merrett 1, FL Mills 7, AN Other 1, JT Parsons 6, JH Rhodes 1, HE Searles
2, JB Shadgett 8, C Sides 2.
Scorers: ER Danks 1, HGH Davoll 1, EJ Jones 1, JB Shadgett 1 (Total 4).
Notes: 4 line-ups, 1 partial line-up and 7 goals missing.

1914-1915

WORLD WAR 1 STARTED IN AUGUST 1914 SO THERE WAS NO LEAGUE FOR THIS SEASON.
WHEN THE WAR ENDED MANY OF THE MEN WHO WERE LATER INDENTIFIED WITH CITY, ATTACHED THEMSELVES TO GLOUCESTER YMCA. TO ALL INTENTS AND PURPOSES IT WAS CITY UNDER A DIFFERENT BANNER. GLOUCESTER YMCA CHANGED BACK TO GLOUCESTER CITY IN 1925.

THE MOMENTOUS ANNOUNCEMENT

GLOUCESTER JOURNAL, SATURDAY, MARCH 10, 1883.

GLOUCESTER ASSOCIATION FOOTBALL CLUB.—A meeting of association players was held on Monday to consider the advisability of forming a club under association rules. The meeting was well attended, and a resolution was passed that a club should be formed, and the election of officers was forthwith proceeded with. Mr W. H. Clarke, British School, was appointed secretary. Already the club has enrolled 25 members.

THE OTHER LEAGUES GLOUCESTER/GLOUCESTER CITY FIRST TEAM PARTICIPATED IN

Gloucester (City) had also entered their first team into these secondary leagues in order to fill out the fixture list. There is an awful lot of information missing. It is as if these games were not worthy of mention and second class!

1898-1899 – MID GLOUCESTERSHIRE LEAGUE
(Gloucester played at Avenue Road Ground (Tuffley Avenue))

15/10/1898 v CHALFORD (H) Won 5-0
HT Robins; WH Hicks, HW Arkell; H Lane, AF Fielding, B Guy; HT Porter, BH Lane, LA Lane, HG Sherwood, FB Fielding.
Scorers: FB Fielding (2), Sherwood, Porter, LA Lane.

24/12/1898 v EBLEY (A) Drew 0-0
(The Citizen missing at the Record Office)

11/03/1899 v BRIMSCOMBE (H) Lost 0-1
G Speck; HW Arkell, SS Harris; RR Sly, JA Oakey, H Lane; FT Rust, AF Fielding, LA Lane, W Long, HT Porter.

08/04/1899 v EBLEY (H) Won 3-0
G Speck; HW Arkell, SS Harris; LA Lane, JA Oakey, RR Sly; HT Porter, AF Fielding, HG Sherwood, FT Rust, JW Stock.
Scorers: AF Fielding, Sherwood, Rust.

15/04/1899 v CHALFORD (A) Won 6-0
(No report in The Citizen)
Scorers: ?. (6 goals missing).

22/04/1899 v BRIMSCOMBE (A) Won 3-1
(Only two players mentioned in The Citizen) AF Fielding, HG Sherwood.
Scorers: AF Fielding (2), Sherwood.

POS	CLUB	P	W	D	L	F	A	PTS
1	GLOUCESTER	6	4	1	1	17	2	9
2	EBLEY	6	3	2	1	13	9	8
3	BRIMSCOMBE	6	2	0	4	12	14	4
4	CHALFORD	6	1	1	4	7	24	3
5	WOTTON-UNDER-EDGE							
		24	10	4	10	49	49	24

Wotton-under-Edge withdrew from league.

Appearances: HW Arkell 3, AF Fielding 4, FB Fielding 1, B Guy 1, SS Harris 2, WH Hicks 1, BH Lane 1, H Lane 2, LA Lane 3, W Long 1, JA Oakey 2, HT Porter 3, HT Robins 1, FT Rust 2, HG Sherwood 3, RR Sly 2, G Speck 2, JW Stock 1.
Scorers: AF Fielding 3, HG Sherwood 3, FB Fielding 2, LA Lane 1, HT Porter 1, FT Rust 1 (Total 11).
Note: 2 line-ups, 1 partial line-up and 6 goals missing.

1899-1900 – MID GLOUCESTERSHIRE LEAGUE
(Gloucester played at Avenue Road Ground (Tuffley Avenue))

07/10/1899 v FOREST GREEN ROVERS (A) Won 6-1
F Hallett; HW Arkell, E Keys; H Lane, JA Oakey, RR Sly; JW Stock, FT Rust, HT Porter, HG Sherwood, W Long.
Scorers: Sherwood (3), Porter (2), Rust.
(This line-up courtesy of The Gloucestershire Echo).

28/10/1899 v CHALFORD (H) Won 8-1
(Only nine players mentioned in The Citizen) F Hallett; HW Arkell, E Keys, JA Oakey, RR Sly, W Long, HT Porter, JW Stock, FT Rust.
Scorers: Long (2), Porter (2), Stock, Arkell, Rust, Oakey.

06/01/1900 v STONEHOUSE (H) Won 7-4
(Only two players mentioned in The Citizen) RR Sly, HT Porter.
Scorers: ?. (7 goals missing).

13/01/1900 v FOREST GREEN ROVERS (H) Won 10-0
(Only six players mentioned in The Citizen) RR Sly, HT Porter, FT Rust, W Shaw, WJ Hart, W Long.
Scorers: Shaw (5), Rust (2), Hart, Sly, Long.

17/03/1900 v EBLEY (A) Won 2-1
F Hallett; HW Arkell, GR Arnold; E Keys, JA Oakey, RR Sly; HT Porter, E May, AF Fielding, FT Rust, JW Stock.
Scorers: May, Rust.
(Line-up and scorers courtesy of Stroud News & Gloucester County Gazette)

31/03/1900 v BRIMSCOMBE (A) Won 5-2
F Hallett; GR Arnold, HW Arkell; RR Sly, E Keys, AF Fielding; J Wakefield, W Shaw, HT Porter, FT Rust, E May.
Scorers: Sly, Rust, Shaw, Keys (pen), May.
(Line-up and scorers courtesy of Stroud News & Gloucester County Gazette)

04/04/1900 v EBLEY (H) Won 7-4
(Only eight players mentioned in The Citizen) AF Fielding, RR Sly, J Wakefield, E Keys, FT Rust, HT Porter, W Shaw, E May.
Scorers: AF Fielding (3), Shaw (3), Rust.

07/04/1900 v STONEHOUSE (A) Won 3-0
F Hallett; HW Arkell, F Pinnegar; AF Fielding, E Keys, RR Sly; J Wakefield, W Shaw, HT Porter, FT Rust, E May.
Scorers: Shaw (2), May.
(This line-up courtesy of The Gloucestershire Echo).

14/04/1900 v CHALFORD (A) Won 1-0
(Only four players mentioned in The Citizen) RR Sly, J Wakefield, HT Porter, E May.
Scorer: Porter.

21/04/1900 v BRIMSCOMBE (H)
Unplayed match.

POS	CLUB	P	W	D	L	F	A	PTS
1	GLOUCESTER +	9	9	0	0	49	13	18
2	EBLEY	10	7	0	3	30	13	14
3	BRIMSCOMBE +	9	3	2	4	17	22	8
4	CHALFORD	10	3	2	5	10	17	8
5	STONEHOUSE	10	1	3	6	16	30	5
6	FOREST GREEN ROVERS	10	2	1	7	9	36	5
		58	25	8	25	131	131	58

+ Brimscombe were down to play on 21/04/1900 but were unable to raise a team. They expressed themselves willing to forfeit the two points.

<u>Appearances</u>: HW Arkell 5, GR Arnold 2, AF Fielding 4, F Hallett 5, WJ Hart 1, E Keys 6, H Lane 1, W Long 3, E May 6, JA Oakey 3, F Pinnegar 1, HT Porter 9, FT Rust 7, W Shaw 4, HG Sherwood 1, RR Sly 9, JW Stock 3, J Wakefield 5.
<u>Scorers</u>: W Shaw 11, FT Rust 7, HT Porter 5, AF Fielding 3, W Long 3, E May 3, HG Sherwood 3, RR Sly 2, HW Arkell 1, WJ Hart 1, E Keys 1, JA Oakey 1, JW Stock 1 (Total 42).
<u>Note</u>: 1 line-up, 5 partial line-ups and 7 goals missing.

1900-1901 – MID GLOUCESTERSHIRE LEAGUE
(Gloucester played at Avenue Road Ground (Tuffley Avenue))

17/11/1900 v BRIMSCOMBE (H) Won 5-1
W Willetts; HW Arkell, GR Arnold; FR Crawley, AF Fielding, T Axford; W Mason, W Shaw, J Wakefield, FT Rust, HT Porter.
Scorers: Rust (3), Shaw, Mason.
(Scorers courtesy of Stroud News & Gloucester County Gazette)
Note: First mention in The Citizen in which the team is named as Gloucester City

15/12/1900 v FOREST GREEN ROVERS (A) Lost 1-4
(No match report in The Citizen)
Scorer: ?. (1 goal missing).

22/12/1900 v WOODCHESTER (A) Won 2-1
(No match report in The Citizen)
Scorers: ?. (2 goals missing).

05/01/1901 v CHALFORD (A) Won 2-0
W Willetts; A Lamb, GR Arnold; FR Crawley, AF Fielding, T Axford; C Wilson, HT Porter, J Wakefield, W Shaw, W Mason.
Scorers: ?. (2 goals missing).
(This line-up courtesy of The Gloucestershire Echo).

30/03/1901 v BRIMSCOMBE (A) Won 6-0
(No match report in The Citizen)
Scorers: ?. (6 goals missing).

06/04/1901 v CHALFORD (H) Won 9-0
W Willetts; HW Arkell, A James; FR Crawley, DE Griffiths, T Axford; FT Rust, W Mason, J Wakefield, HT Porter (only ten players used).

Scorers: Mason (4), Griffiths (2), Wakefield (2), Rust.
13/04/1901 v EBLEY (A) Won 2-0
(Only three players mentioned in The Citizen) W Willetts; W Mason, FT Rust.
Scorers: Mason (2).

18/04/1901 v EBLEY (H) Won 5-0
W Willetts; H Lane, F Pinnegar; T Axford, FR Crawley, W Shaw; W Mason, HT Porter, J Wakefield, FT Rust, C Wilson.
Scorers: Shaw (3), Rust, Mason.
(This line-up courtesy of The Gloucestershire Echo).

20/04/1901 v FOREST GREEN ROVERS (H) Won 5-0
W Willetts; HW Arkell, F Pinnegar; FR Crawley, E Keys, T Axford; HT Porter, W Mason, W Shaw, FT Rust, C Wilson.
Scorers: Shaw (2), Mason, Rust, Crawley.

27/04/1901 v WOODCHESTER (H) Won 2-0
W Willetts; AF Fielding, F Pinnegar; TH Rust, T Axford, C Wilson; WJ Hart, W Shaw, W Mason, FT Rust, HT Porter.
Scorers: Shaw, FT Rust.

POS	CLUB	P	W	D	L	F	A	PTS
1	GLOUCESTER	10	9	0	1	39	6	18
2	BRIMSCOMBE							
3	CHALFORD							
4	FOREST GREEN ROVERS							
5	WOODCHESTER							
6	WYCLIFFE COLLEGE							

Wycliffe College withdrew from league.
Gloucester champions but no league table found.

Appearances: HW Arkell 3, GR Arnold 2, TE Axford 6, FR Crawley 5, AF Fielding 3, DE Griffiths 1, WJ Hart 1, A James 1, E Keys 1, A Lamb 1, H Lane 1, W Mason 7, F Pinnegar 3, HT Porter 6, FT Rust 6, TH Rust 1, W Shaw 5, J Wakefield 4, W Willetts 7, C Wilson 4.
Scorers: W Mason 9, W Shaw 7, FT Rust 7, DE Griffiths 2, J Wakefield 2, FR Crawley 1 (Total 28).
Note: 3 line-ups, 2 partial line-ups and 11 goals missing.

1906-1907 – CHELTENHAM AND DISTRICT LEAGUE – FIRST DIVISION
(Gloucester City played at Budding's Field)

06/10/1906 v TEWKESBURY TOWN (H) Won 3-2
W Willetts; AS Keeping, FE Quixley; J Hill, AH Smith, AV Boughton; EF Davy, CH Haddon, WD Niblett, W Smith, JM Baldwin.
Scorers: W Smith (2, 1pen), Niblett.

15/12/1906 v TEWKESBURY TOWN (A) Won 1-0
W Willetts; WD Vinson, FE Quixley; GA Vinson, AV Boughton, AH Smith; CH Haddon, JM Baldwin, N Squier, H Smith, W Smith.
Scorer: Squier.

29/12/1906 v WINCHCOMBE TOWN (H) Won 6-0
W Willetts; EF Davy, FE Quixley; GA Vinson, AV Boughton, C Bain; BG Harris, AE Bland, Wilfred Nicholls, OJA Carter, JM Baldwin.
Scorers: Bland (4), Baldwin, Nicholls.

05/01/1907 v CHELTENHAM TOWN (A) Won 1-0
W Willetts; WD Vinson, EF Davy; GA Vinson, AH Smith, FE Quixley; W Smith, AE Bland, Wilfred Nicholls, AV Boughton, JM Baldwin.
Scorer: Bland.

02/02/1907 v CHELTENHAM TOWN (H) Won 3-2
W Willetts; WD Vinson, FE Quixley; GA Vinson, AV Boughton, AH Smith; CH Haddon, H Smith, JM Baldwin, AJ Carter, W Smith.
Scorers: Carter (2), H Smith.

09/02/1907 v WINCHCOMBE TOWN (A) Drew 1-1
W Willetts; WD Vinson, FE Quixley; GA Vinson, AV Boughton, AH Smith; CH Haddon, H Smith, N. Squier, JM Baldwin, W Smith.
Scorer: Squier.
(This line-up courtesy of The Gloucestershire Echo).

23/03/1907 v SAINT PAUL'S UNITED (H) Won 2-0
W Willetts; EF Davy, FE Quixley; GA Vinson, AV Boughton, AH Smith; CH Haddon, AJ Carter, N Squier, AE Kent, W Smith.
Scorers: Squier (2).

06/04/1907 v SAINT PAUL'S UNITED (A) Won 3-1
W Willetts; EF Davy, FE Quixley; GA Vinson, AV Boughton, C Bain; H Smith, AJ Carter, AH Smith, AE Kent, W Smith.
Scorers: Kent, Carter, ?. (1 goal missing).

POS	CLUB	P	W	D	L	F	A	PTS
1	GLOUCESTER CITY	8	7	1	0	20	6	15
2	SAINT PAUL'S UNITED	5	1	1	3	6	9	3
3	WINCHCOMBE TOWN	4	1	1	2	2	10	3
4	CHELTENHAM TOWN	4	1	0	3	5	6	2
5	TEWKESBURY TOWN	3	0	1	2	3	5	1
		24	10	4	10	36	36	24

Table incomplete. No table in either The Citizen or The Gloucestershire Echo. Based only on results I could find.

Appearances: C Bain 2, JM Baldwin 6, AE Bland 2, AV Boughton 8, AJ Carter 3, OJA Carter 1, EF Davy 5, CH Haddon 5, BG Harris 1, J Hill 1, AS Keeping 1, AE Kent 2, WD Niblett 1, Wilfred Nicholls 2, FE Quixley 8, AH Smith 7, H Smith 4, W Smith 7, N Squier 3, GA Vinson 7, WD Vinson 4, W Willetts 8.
Scorers: AE Bland 5, N Squier 4, AJ Carter 3, W Smith 2, JM Baldwin 1, AE Kent 1, WD Niblett 1, Wilfred Nicholls 1, H Smith 1 (Total 19).
Note: 1 goal missing.

GLOUCESTER CITY (WINNERS).

Back row.—G. A. Vinson, E. F. Davy, B. Boughton, W. Willetts, A. H. Smith, F. E. Quixley.
Front row.—C. H. Haddon, H. Smith, A. Carter, A. E. Kent, W. Smith.

1909-1910 – CHELTENHAM AND DISTRICT LEAGUE – FIRST DIVISION
(Gloucester City played at Budding's Field)

25/09/1909 v WINCHCOMBE TOWN (H) Won 3-2
WC Vickery; W Ingles, FE Taylor; GA Vinson, AH Smith, J Hill; AE Bland, F Haynes, WA Jarman, AJ Carter, AE Kent.
Scorers: Bland, Jarman, Haynes.

09/10/1909 v EVESHAM UNITED (H) Drew 2-2
WC Vickery; JG Eldridge, W Ingles; GA Vinson, A Watts, J Hill; L Bathurst, AE Bland, WA Jarman, W Smith, AE Kent.
Scorers: own goal, Watts.

20/11/1909 v TEWKESBURY TOWN (A) Won 4-2
WC Vickery; W Ingles, JG Eldridge; GA Vinson, AH Smith, J Hill; S Cook, N Squier, A Watts, W Smith, AE Kent.
Scorers: Squier (3), Kent.

18/12/1909 v TEWKESBURY TOWN (H) Drew 2-2
WC Vickery; W Ingles, LA Carleton; GA Vinson, FE Quixley, J Hill; AL Haydon, A Watts, WA Jarman, W Smith, AE Kent.
Scorers: Watts, Haydon.

24/02/1910 v CHELTENHAM TOWN (A) Lost 1-2
WC Vickery; W Ingles; GA Vinson, A Watts, CG Carter; S Cook, AH Smith, WA Jarman, W Smith, AE Kent (only ten players used).
Scorer: W Smith.

13/03/1910 v EVESHAM UNITED (A) Lost 0-3
WC Vickery; LA Carleton; GA Vinson, AH Smith, CG Carter; S Cook, A Watts, WA Jarman, W Smith, AE Kent (only 10 players used).

26/03/1910 v CHELTENHAM TOWN (H) Drew 3-3
GB Brace; LA Carleton, W Ingles; GA Vinson, A Watts, ? Acton; AH Smith, WA Jarman, AE Kent, JT Parsons.
Scorers: Jarman (2), Kent.

09/04/1910 v SAINT PAUL'S UNITED (H) match abandoned, visitors never turned up. The following eleven selected.
WC Vickery; W Ingles, LA Carleton; GA Vinson, A Watts, CG Carter; S Cook, AH Smith,
WA Jarman,
W Smith, AE Kent.

23/04/1910 v SAINT PAUL'S UNITED (A) Drew 1-1
WC Vickery; W Ingles, LA Carleton; TT Vickery, FE Quixley, J Hill; CE Brown, FE Taylor, S Cook, JT Parsons, C Carter.
Scorer: Parsons.
(This result also counted for The North Gloucestershire League. Played 35 minutes each way).

v WINCHCOMBE TOWN (A) Drew 1-1
missing

POS	CLUB	P	W	D	L	F	A	PTS
1	CHELTENHAM TOWN	7	3	3	1	12	11	9
2	GLOUCESTER CITY +	9	2	5	2	17	18	9
3	SAINT PAUL'S UNITED +	7	2	3	2	11	7	7
4	TEWKESBURY TOWN	6	2	2	2	8	12	6
5	EVESHAM UNITED	4	2	1	1	9	6	5
6	WINCHCOMBE TOWN	3	0	0	3	3	6	0
		36	11	14	11	60	60	36

+ Match abandoned
Table incomplete. No table in either The Citizen or The Gloucestershire Echo. Based only on results I could find.

Appearances: ? Acton 1, L Bathurst 1, AE Bland 2, GB Brace 1, CE Brown 1, LA Carleton 4, AJ Carter 1, C Carter 1, CG Carter 2, S Cook 4, JG Eldridge 2, AL Haydon 1, F Haynes 1, J Hill 5, W Ingles 7, WA Jarman 6, AE Kent 7, JT Parsons 2, FE Quixley 2, AH Smith 5, W Smith 5, N Squier 1, FE Taylor 2, TT Vickery 1, WC Vickery 7, GA Vinson 7, A Watts 6.
Scorers: WA Jarman 3, N Squier 3, AE Kent 2, A Watts 2, AE Bland 1, AL Haydon 1, F Haynes 1, JT Parsons 1, W Smith 1, own goal 1 (Total 16).
Notes: 1 line-up and 1 goal missing.

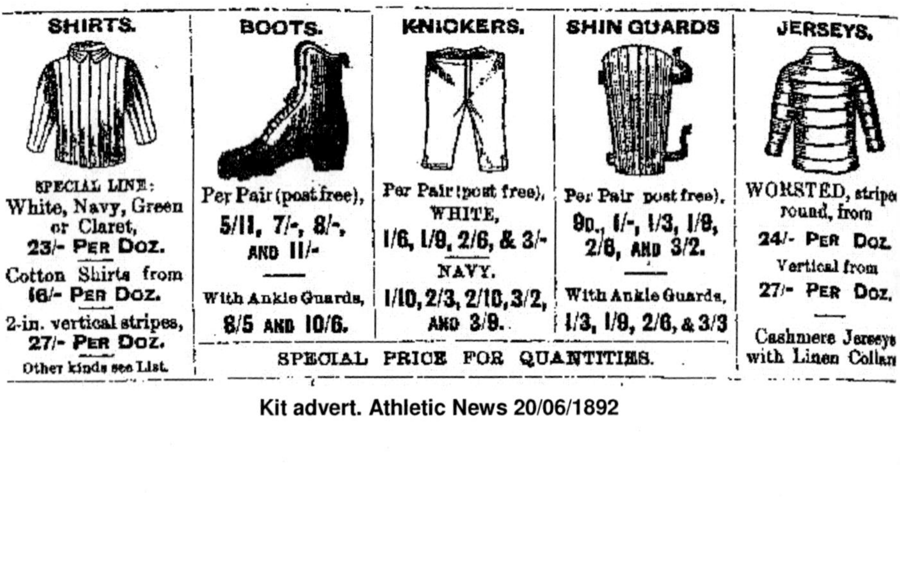

SHIRTS.	BOOTS.	KNICKERS.	SHIN GUARDS.	JERSEYS.
SPECIAL LINE: White, Navy, Green or Claret, 23/- PER DOZ. Cotton Shirts from 16/- PER DOZ. 2-in. vertical stripes, 27/- PER DOZ. Other kinds see List.	Per Pair (post free), 5/11, 7/-, 8/-, AND 11/- — With Ankle Guards, 8/5 AND 10/6.	Per Pair (post free), WHITE, 1/6, 1/9, 2/6, & 3/- NAVY. 1/10, 2/3, 2/10, 3/2, AND 3/9.	Per Pair post free, 9D., 1/-, 1/3, 1/8, 2/6, AND 3/2. — With Ankle Guards, 1/3, 1/9, 2/6, & 3/3	WORSTED, stripe round, from 24/- PER DOZ. Vertical from 27/- PER DOZ. Cashmere Jerseys with Linen Collar

SPECIAL PRICE FOR QUANTITIES.

Kit advert. Athletic News 20/06/1892

GLOUCESTER/GLOUCESTER YMCA/GLOUCESTER CITY PLAYERS 1893 TO 1914 (TOTAL = 186)
ONLY PLAYERS WHO PARTICIPATED IN LEAGUE GAMES APPEAR HERE

Qu1 = Jan to Mar, Qu2 = Apr to Jun, Qu3 = Jul to Sep, Qu4 = Oct to Dec

Club Records: Obviously incomplete. Only found if I happen to see their names on other team selections or if an article was written about an individual which was rare.

No League participation in the following seasons: 1896/97, 1901/02, 1904/05, 1905/06, 1910/11, 1911/12 and 1912/13.

ACTON, ? (WH)
1909/10 1 app 0 gls
TOTAL 1 app 0 gls

ALLEN, E.E (IF)
1913/14 6 apps 0 gls
TOTAL 6 apps 0 gls
Note: Also played for Gloucester YMCA 1919/20.

ARKELL, Henry Witcomb (IF/FB)
b. Qu3 1878 Gloucester d. ?
1897/98 4 apps 2 gls
1898/99 12 apps 3 gls
1899/00 12 apps 2 gls
1900/01 9 apps 0 gls
1902/03 8 apps 0 gls
1903/04 2 apps 0 gls
TOTAL 47 apps 7 gls
Note: Joint Club Secretary 1902-03. Played for Gloucester 1896/97.

ARNOLD, G.R (FB)
1899/00 2 apps 0 gls
1900/01 4 apps 0 gls
1903/04 2 apps 1 gl
TOTAL 8 apps 1 gl

AXFORD, Thomas E (WH)
b. 1873 Monkton, Wilts. d. ?
1900/01 12 apps 0 gls
TOTAL 12 apps 0 gls

BAIN, C (HB)
1906/07 2 apps 0 gls
TOTAL 2 apps 0 gls

BALDWIN, J.M (IF)
1906/07 11 apps 5 gls
TOTAL 11 apps 5 gls

BARNARD, H (FB)
1894/95 1 app 0 gls
TOTAL 1 app 0 gls
Note: Played for Gloucester 1889/90, 1890/91, 1892/93.

BARNES, C (IF)
1909/10 1 app 0 gls
TOTAL 1 app 0 gls
Note: Played for Gloucester City 1906/07.

BARRETT, Archibald Manning (IF)
b. Qu1 1893 Gloucester d. 23/03/1916 Merville, France
1913/14 1 app 0 gls
TOTAL 1 app 0 gls
Note: Killed in action WW1.

BATHURST, L (IF)
1909/10 2 apps 0 gls
TOTAL 2 apps 0 gls
Club Record: Tewkesbury Abbey, Gloucester City +.

"BEDMAN", W (CF)
1894/95 1 app 0 gls
TOTAL 1 app 0 gls

BENBOW, ? (IF)
1909/10 1 app 0 gls
TOTAL 1 app 0 gls

BLAKE, W.T (GK)
1907/08 5 apps 0 gls
TOTAL 5 apps 0 gls
Club Record: Cheltenham Town, Gloucester City +.

BLAND, A.E (IF)
1906/07 2 apps 5 gls
TOTAL 2 apps 5 gls

BOONAVALLE, ? (IF)
1903/04 1 app 1 gl
TOTAL 1 app 1 gl
Note: Surname could be Boonaville.

BOTTOMLEY, F.E (W)
1907/08 2 apps 0 gls
TOTAL 2 apps 0 gls

BOUGHTON, Albert Victor (Bert) (WH)
b. Qu1 1885 Droitwich, Worcs. d. ?
1906/07 13 apps 1 gl
1907/08 13 apps 0 gls
1908/09 1 app 0 gls
TOTAL 27 apps 1 gl

BRACE, G.B (GK)
1909/10 3 apps 0 gls
TOTAL 3 apps 0 gls
Note: Played for Gloucester City 1907/08, 1908/09.

BRETHERTON, Charles Archibald (FB)
b. Qu3 1886 Gloucester d. ?
1913/14 7 apps 0 gls
TOTAL 7 apps 0 gls
Note: Club Captain 1913-1914. Also played for Gloucester YMCA 1919/20, 1920/21.

BROWN, C.E (WH)
1909/10 2 apps 0 gls
TOTAL 2 apps 0 gls
Note: Played for Gloucester City 1908/09.

BROWN, W.A (HB)
1897/98 3 apps 0 gls
TOTAL 3 apps 0 gls
Note: Played for Gloucester 1896/97.

BURT, ? (FB)
1894/95 1 app 0 gls
TOTAL 1 app 0 gls

BUTLER, L (IF)
1908/09 1 app 0 gls
TOTAL 1 app 0 gls

BYGRAVE, P (HB)
1913/14 1 app 0 gls
TOTAL 1 app 0 gls

CARELY, F (HB)
1895/96 1 app 0 gls
TOTAL 1 app 0 gls

CARLETON, L.A (FB)
1909/10 11 apps 0 gls
TOTAL 11 apps 0 gls

CARTER, Alfred J (Alf) (IF)
1906/07 4 apps 3 gls
1907/08 14 apps 10 gls
1908/09 6 apps 2 gls
1909/10 1 app 0 gls
TOTAL 25 app 15 gls

CARTER, C (W)
1909/10 3 apps 0 gls
TOTAL 3 apps 0 gls
Note: Played for Gloucester City 1907/08.

CARTER, C.G (WH)
1909/10 7 apps 3 gls
TOTAL 7 apps 3 gls

CARTER, L.H (FB)
1894/95 1 app 0 gls
TOTAL 1 app 0 gls
Note: Played for Gloucester 1889/90.

CARTER, Oliver John Arthur (Olly) (IF)
b. Qu1 1885 Gloucester d. 13/01/1953
1906/07 1 app 0 gls
TOTAL 1 app 0 gls
Note: Club Secretary 1909-10.

CLARK, T (HB)
1893/94 2 apps 0 gls
TOTAL 2 apps 0 gls

CLUTTERBUCK, George Charles (IF)
b. Qu2 1875 Clifton, Bristol, Glos. d. ?
1894/95 3 apps 0 gls
1895/96 10 apps 3 gls
TOTAL 13 apps 3 gls

COOK, S (W)
1908/09 1 app 0 gls
1909/10 12 apps 4 gls
TOTAL 13 app 4 gls

CORBETT, F (HB)
1913/14 1 app 0 gls
TOTAL 1 app 0 gls

CRAGG, A.C (HB)
1893/94 13 apps 0 gls
1894/95 15 apps 1 gl
1895/96 9 apps 0 gls
TOTAL 37 apps 1 gl
Note: Played for Gloucester 1892/93, 1896/97.

CRAWLEY, Frank R (WH)
b. 1883 Hull, Yorks. d. ?
1900/01 10 apps 1 gl
1902/03 6 apps 0 gls
1903/04 8 apps 1 gl
TOTAL 24 apps 2 gls
Note: Club Secretary 1903-05.

CROUCH, Francis E.A (W)
b. 1879 St.Blazey, Cornwall d. ?
1906/07 1 app 1 gl
TOTAL 1 app 1 gl
Club Record: Plymouth Phoenix/Argyle, Loughborough Corinthians, Saint Michael's, Gloucester City +.

DANIELLS, H (W)
1895/96 1 app 1 gl
TOTAL 1 app 1 gl
Club Record: Gloucester, Gloucester Post Office +.
Note: Played for Gloucester 1896/97.

DANKS, E.R (W)
1913/14 7 apps 1 gl
TOTAL 7 apps 1 gl

DAVOLL, H.G.H (W/GK)
1909/10 1 app 0 gls
1913/14 6 apps 1 gl
TOTAL 7 apps 1 gl
Club Record: Gloucester City, Gloucester YMCA +.
Note: Played in goal for YMCA 1913/14.

DAVY, Ernest F (FB)
b. 1880 Gloucester d. ?
1902/03 2 apps 0 gls
1903/04 8 apps 0 gls
1906/07 8 apps 0 gls
1907/08 14 apps 2 gls
TOTAL 32 apps 2 gls
Club Record: YMCA Pioneer Club, Gloucester City, Sir Thomas Rich's Old Boys, Gloucester City +.
Note: Club Captain 1906-08.

DEE, F.W (FB)
1906/07 1 app 0 gls
TOTAL 1 app 0 gls

DEE, W.H (FB)
1902/03 1 app 0 gls
TOTAL 1 app 0 gls

DUDBRIDGE, L.F (IF)
1913/14 5 apps 0 gls
TOTAL 5 apps 0 gls

DURRETT, C (IF)
1909/10 1 app 2 gls
1913/14 2 apps 0 gls
TOTAL 3 app 2 gls
Club Record: Gloucester City, Gloucester YMCA +.

EDDOWES, C.F.B (CH)
1902/03 6 apps 0 gls
1903/04 8 apps 0 gls
TOTAL 14 apps 0 gls
Note: Played for Gloucester City 1907/08.

ELDRIDGE, J.G (FB)
1909/10 3 apps 0 gls
TOTAL 3 apps 0 gls

ELSE, S.O (WH)
1902/03 1 app 0 gls
TOTAL 1 app 0 gls

FIELDING, Arthur Fitton (F/WH/FB)
b. Qu1 1877 Gloucester d. ?
1893/94 4 apps 0 gls
1894/95 15 apps 6 gls
1895/96 17 apps 0 gls
1897/98 3 apps 3 gls
1898/99 13 apps 7 gls
1899/00 10 apps 5 gls
1900/01 8 apps 0 gls
1902/03 5 apps 0 gls
1903/04 7 apps 1 gl
TOTAL 82 apps 22 gls
Club Record: Gloucester, Bristol City (0) +.
Note: Club Captain 1897-1900. Brother of Frank Fielding and Samuel Fielding. Played for Gloucester 1896/97.

FIELDING, Frank Berry (F)
b. Qu3 1872 Gloucester d. ?
1893/94 15 apps 8 gls
1894/95 17 apps 12 gls
1895/96 16 apps 11 gls
1897/98 3 apps 5 gls
1898/99 2 app 2 gls
TOTAL 53 apps 38 gls
Club Record: Gloucester, Bristol City (0) +.
Note: Club Captain 1893-94. Brother of Arthur Fielding and Samuel Fielding. Played for Gloucester 1889/90, 1890/91, 1891/92, 1892/93.

FIELDING, Samuel John (IF)
b. Qu4 1882 Gloucester d. ?
1902/03 1 app 0 gls
TOTAL 1 app 0 gls
Note: Brother of Frank Fielding and Arthur Fielding.

FOWLER, G.W (IF)
1902/03 5 apps 0 gls
TOTAL 5 apps 0 gls

FOWLER, H.O (FB)
1893/94 2 apps 0 gls
TOTAL 2 apps 0 gls

FOWLER, R.C (FB)
1894/95 8 apps 0 gls
1895/96 5 apps 0 gls
TOTAL 13 apps 0 gls
Club Record: Lancing College, Gloucester +.

FRANKLIN, J (W)
1895/96 2 apps 0 gls
TOTAL 2 apps 0 gls

FRITH, Arthur P (IF)
b. abt 1877 Gloucester d. ?
1894/95 1 app 0 gls
1895/96 10 apps 0 gls
TOTAL 11 app 0 gls
Note: Played for Gloucester 1896/97, 1898/99.

GARDNER, W.T (W)
1897/98 1 app 0 gls
TOTAL 1 app 0 gls
Note: Played for Gloucester 1892/93.

GOODWIN, A.E (FB)
1894/95 5 apps 0 gls
1895/96 3 apps 0 gls
TOTAL 8 apps 0 gls

GREEN, H.D (CF)
1895/96 3 apps 2 gls
TOTAL 3 apps 2 gls

GREEN, R.N (FB)
1893/94 7 apps 0 gls
TOTAL 7 apps 0 gls
Note: Played for Gloucester 1892/93.

GRIFFITHS, David E (CH)
b. 1872 Saint Dogmaels, Pembrokeshire, Wales d. ?
1900/01 2 apps 2 gls
1902/03 1 app 0 gls
TOTAL 3 apps 2 gls

GUY, Bert (HB)
1898/99 2 apps 1 gl
TOTAL 2 apps 1 gl

HADDON, C.H (IF)
1906/07 11 apps 2 gls
1907/08 5 apps 1 gl
1908/09 1 app 0 gls
TOTAL 17 apps 3 gls

HALE, H.W (IF)
1907/08 2 apps 0 gls
TOTAL 2 apps 0 gls

HALLETT, Frank (GK)
b. 1878 Kingswood, Glos. d. ?
1899/00 12 apps 0 gls
TOTAL 12 apps 0 gls

HARRIS, B.G (HB)
1906/07 1 app 0 gls
TOTAL 1 app 0 gls
Club Record: Gloucester City, Gloucester City Albions +.
Note: Played for Gloucester City 1907/08.

HARRIS, H (CF)
1895/96 5 apps 1 gl
TOTAL 5 apps 1 gl

HARRIS, Sidney Samuel (Sid) (FB)
b. Qu4 1877 Gloucester d. ?
1897/98 3 apps 0 gls
1898/99 9 apps 0 gls
TOTAL 12 apps 0 gls

HART, W.J (IF)
1899/00 3 apps 2 gls
1900/01 1 app 0 gls
TOTAL 4 apps 2 gls

HARVEY, Rev. J.H (HB)
1893/94 7 apps 0 gls
TOTAL 7 apps 0 gls
Club Record: Gloucester, Cheltenham Town +.
Note: Played for Gloucester 1891/92, 1892/93.

HAWKINS, J (GK)
1902/03 1 app 0 gls
TOTAL 1 app 0 gls
Note: Played for Gloucester City 1903/04.

HAYDON, A.L (IF)
1907/08 1 app 0 gls
1909/10 1 app 1 gl
TOTAL 2 apps 1 gl

HAYNES, F (IF)
1909/10 1 app 1 gl
TOTAL 1 app 1 gl

HICKS, Walter H (FB)
1895/96 3 apps 0 gls
1897/98 3 apps 0 gls
1898/99 3 apps 0 gls
TOTAL 9 apps 0 gls
Note: Played for Gloucester 1896/97.

HILL, J (WH)
1906/07 1 app 0 gls
1907/08 3 apps 1 gl
1908/09 13 apps 1 gl
1909/10 11 apps 0 gls
TOTAL 28 apps 2 gls
Club Record: Exeter City, Gloucester City +.

HOARE, A.S (GK)
1903/04 2 apps 0 gls
TOTAL 2 apps 0 gls
Club Record: Gloucester Thursday, Gloucester City +.

HOITT, A.C (HB)
1893/94 4 apps 0 gls
TOTAL 4 apps 0 gls

INGLES, W (FB)
1909/10 17 apps 2 gls
TOTAL 17 apps 2 gls

JAMES, Allan (FB)
b. 1883 Goodrich, Herefordshire d. ?
1900/01 2 apps 0 gls
TOTAL 2 apps 0 gls

JAMES, E.T (IF)
1895/96 3 apps 0 gls
TOTAL 3 apps 0 gls
Note: Played for Gloucester 1896/97.

JARMAN, W.A (CF)
1908/09 10 apps 16 gls
1909/10 16 apps 8 gls
TOTAL 26 apps 24 gls

JESSOP, A (CF)
1893/94 1 app 1 gl
TOTAL 1 app 1 gl

JESSOP, Gilbert Laird (CF)
b. 19/05/1874 Cheltenham, Glos. d.
11/05/1955 Fordington, Dorset
1895/96 2 apps 0 gls
TOTAL 2 apps 0 gls
Club Record: Gloucester, Cheltenham, Cambridge University, The Casuals +.
Note: Gilbert Jessop played cricket for Gloucestershire CCC 1894-1914, Cambridge University 1896-1899 and London County 1900-1903 and represented England 18 times between 1899 and 1912. He also played rugby for Gloucester RFC and Clifton RFC.

JOHNSON, A.E (HB)
b. c1873 d. ?
1893/94 1 app 0 gls
TOTAL 1 app 0 gls
Note: Played for Gloucester 1889/90, 1890/91, 1891/92, 1892/93.

JONES, E.J (CF)
1913/14 7 apps 1 gl
TOTAL 7 apps 1 gl

JONES, W (GK)
1903/04 2 apps 0 gls
TOTAL 2 apps 0 gls
Note: Played for Gloucester 1890/91, 1898/99.

KEEPING, A.S (FB)
1906/07 1 app 0 gls
TOTAL 1 app 0 gls

KENT, Albert Edward (W)
b. Qu4 1882 Gloucester d. ?
1906/07 4 apps 2 gls
1907/08 14 apps 4 gls
1908/09 13 apps 3 gls
1909/10 16 apps 3 gls
TOTAL 47 apps 12 gls

KENT, S.J.F (GK)
1893/94 15 apps 0 gls
TOTAL 15 apps 0 gls
Club Record: Weymouth, Gloucester.

KEYS, E (WH)
1899/00 12 apps 2 gls
1900/01 2 apps 0 gls
1903/04 2 apps 0 gls
TOTAL 16 apps 2 gls
Club Record: Gloucester Teachers, Gloucester City +.

LAMB, A (FB)
1900/01 1 app 0 gls
1903/04 1 app 0 gls
TOTAL 2 apps 0 gls

LAMBE, W.H (FB)
1900/01 1 app 0 gls
TOTAL 1 app 0 gls

LANE, B.H (IF)
1898/99 5 apps 0 gls
TOTAL 5 apps 0 gls

LANE, Herbert (HB)
b. 1880 Gloucester d. ?
1898/99 9 apps 0 gls
1899/00 2 apps 1 gl
1900/01 2 apps 0 gls
TOTAL 13 apps 1 gl
Note: Brother of Lionel Lane.

LANE, J.B (HB)
1913/14 4 apps 0 gls
TOTAL 4 apps 0 gls

LANE, Lionel A (W)
b. 1878 Gloucester d. ?
1897/98 2 apps 1 gl
1898/99 11 apps 5 gls
TOTAL 13 apps 6 gls
Club Record: Gloucester, Gloucester City Albions +.
Note: Club Secretary 1898-99. Brother of Herbert Lane.

LEWIS, ? (IF)
1903/04 1 app 1 gl
TOTAL 1 app 1 gl

LLEWELLYN, W (IF)
1899/00 1 app 1 gl
TOTAL 1 app 1 gl

LONG, W (Nobby) (W)
1898/99 3 apps 0 gls
1899/00 5 app 3 gls
TOTAL 8 apps 3 gls

LUCAS, Oliver James (IF)
b. Qu3 1887 Gloucester d. ?
1907/08 12 apps 5 gls
TOTAL 12 apps 5 gls

MACKAY, ? (CH)
1895/96 1 app 0 gls
TOTAL 1 app 0 gls

MANSFIELD, ? (FB)
1894/95 1 app 0 gls
TOTAL 1 app 0 gls

MASON, ? (IF)
1893/94 1 app 0 gls
TOTAL 1 app 0 gls

MASON, W (W)
1900/01 15 apps 9 gls
TOTAL 15 apps 9 gls

MATTHEWS, W.G (W)
1893/94 8 apps 2 gls
1894/95 2 apps 0 gls
TOTAL 10 apps 2 gls
Note: Played for Gloucester 1890/91, 1892/93.

MAY, E (IF)
1899/00 5 apps 3 gls
TOTAL 5 apps 3 gls

McFARLANE, J.M (FB)
1913/14 6 apps 0 gls
TOTAL 6 apps 0 gls
Note: There is a JM McFarlane on the War Memorial, Gloucester.

MERRETT, J.H (HB)
1913/14 1 app 0 gls
TOTAL 1 app 0 gls

MILLS, F.L (W)
1913/14 7 apps 0 gls
TOTAL 7 apps 0 gls
Note: Also played for Gloucester YMCA 1919/20, 1920/21.

MORLEY, R.F (CH)
1899/00 1 app 0 gls
TOTAL 1 app 0 gls

MORRIS, F.M (FB)
1893/94 1 app 0 gls
1894/95 4 apps 1 gl
1895/96 1 app 0 gls
TOTAL 6 apps 1 gl
Note: Played for Gloucester 1889/90, 1891/92.

MURRAY, C (GK)
1903/04 1 app 0 gls
TOTAL 1 app 0 gls

NIBLETT, William Douglas (IF)
b. Qu1 1885 Horsley, Glos. d. ?
1906/07 2 apps 1 gl
TOTAL 2 apps 1 gl

NICHOLLS, H (WH)
1899/00 1 app 0 gls
TOTAL 1 app 0 gls

NICHOLLS, Wilfred T (CF)
b. 1885 Gloucester d. ?
1906/07 2 apps 1 gl
TOTAL 2 apps 1 gl
Note: Brother of Walter Nicholls.

NORRINGTON, C.H (HB)
1893/94 1 app 0 gls
TOTAL 1 app 0 gls

OAKEY, John Arthur (HB)
b. Qu1 1875 Gloucester d. aft. 1953
1895/96 1 app 0 gls
1897/98 3 apps 1 gl
1898/99 8 apps 0 gls
1899/00 3 apps 1 gl
TOTAL 15 apps 2 gls
Club Record: Gloucester, Gloucester YMRIS, Gloucester Teachers, Gloucester +.
Note: Played for Gloucester 1896/97.

PALMER, R.M (FB)
1908/09 1 app 0 gls
TOTAL 1 app 0 gls
Note: Played for Gloucester City 1907/08.

PARKER, Albert (IF)
1902/03 6 apps 5 gls
1903/04 10 apps 5 gls
TOTAL 16 apps 10 gls

PARKER, J.M (HB)
1894/95 3 apps 0 gls
TOTAL 3 apps 0 gls

PARSONS, J.T (IF)
1909/10 7 apps 2 gls
1913/14 6 apps 0 gls
TOTAL 13 apps 2 gls
Club Record: Gloucester City, Gloucester YMCA +.
Note: Played for Gloucester City 1908/09.

PEARCE, F (IF)
1895/96 1 app 0 gls
TOTAL 1 app 0 gls

PECKOVER, L (CH)
1902/03 1 app 0 gls
TOTAL 1 app 0 gls
Note: Played for Gloucester City 1903/04.

PENNINGTON, ? (WH)
1893/94 1 app 0 gls
TOTAL 1 app 0 gls

PETTEY, C (IF)
1894/95 1 app 0 gls
1895/96 2 apps 1 gl
1897/98 1 app 0 gls
TOTAL 4 apps 1 gl

PINNEGAR, Frederick (FB)
b. 1876 Wotton-under-Edge, Glos. d. ?
1899/00 7 apps 0 gls
1900/01 4 apps 0 gls
TOTAL 11 apps 0 gls
Club Record: Gloucester, Saint Michael's +.

PITT, William Thomas (HB)
b. 1875 Battersea, London d. ?
1894/95 5 apps 0 gls
1895/96 2 apps 0 gls
TOTAL 7 apps 0 gls
Club Record: Gloucester, Gloucester Post Office +.
Note: Played for Gloucester 1896/97.

PORTER, Henry T (CF)
b. 1871 Bristol, Glos d. ?
1895/96 1 app 0 gls
1897/98 6 apps 10 gls
1898/99 12 apps 6 gls
1899/00 18 apps 12 gls
1900/01 13 apps 3 gls
TOTAL 50 apps 31 gls
Note: Played for Gloucester City 1902/03.

POWELL, J.O.T (CF)
1893/94 1 app 1 gl
TOTAL 1 app 1 gl
Note: Played for Gloucester 1891/92, 1892/93, 1894/95.

QUIXLEY, Frederick E (FB)
b. 1886 Luton, Beds. d. ?
1906/07 14 apps 0 gls
1907/08 12 apps 0 gls
1908/09 13 apps 0 gls
1909/10 4 apps 0 gls
TOTAL 43 apps 0 gls
Club Record: Gloucester City, Gloucester City Albion +.

RADFORD, J (IF)
1894/95 2 apps 0 gls
1895/96 1 app 0 gls
TOTAL 3 apps 0 gls
Note: Played for Gloucester 1896/97.

RHODES, J.H (GK)
1913/14 1 app 0 gls
TOTAL 1 app 0 gls

RICH, S.T (CF)
1899/00 1 app 0 gls
TOTAL 1 app 0 gls

RICHARDSON, Harold L (Harry) (W)
b. 1873 Upton-on-Severn, Worcs. d. ?
1902/03 3 apps 0 gls
1903/04 2 apps 0 gls
TOTAL 5 apps 0 gls

ROBINS, H.T (IF/GK)
1893/94 15 apps 2 gls
1894/95 7 apps 2 gls
1895/96 3 apps 0 gls
1898/99 1 app 0 gls
TOTAL 26 apps 4 gls
Note: Played for Gloucester 1891/92, 1892/93, 1896/97.

ROMANS, Francis Charles J (W)
b. Qu2 1882 Gloucester d. ?
1902/03 4 apps 0 gls
TOTAL 4 apps 0 gls

RUST, Frederick Thomas (Fred) (IF)
b. Qu3 1879 Gloucester d. ?
1898/99 6 apps 4 gls
1899/00 14 apps 9 gls
1900/01 8 apps 7 gls
1902/03 8 apps 3 gls
1903/04 9 apps 15 gls
TOTAL 45 apps 38 gls
Club Record: Gloucester, Saint Michael's, Gloucester City, Gloucester Thursday +.
Note: Club Captain 1900-04. Brother of Thomas Rust. Played for Gloucester City 1906/07.

RUST, Thomas Henry (Tom) (CH)
b. 03/03/1881 Gloucester d. 09/08/1962 Gloucester
1900/01 1 app 0 gls
1903/04 9 apps 1 gl
TOTAL 10 apps 1 gl
Club Record: Gloucester City, Gloucester Thursday +.
Note: Brother of Frederick Rust. Played for Gloucester City 1902/03. Played cricket for Gloucestershire CCC 1914.

SAUNDERS, G
1897/98 1 app 1 gl
TOTAL 1 app 1 gl

SCOTT, Herbert Harger (HB)
b. Qu1 1873 Stone, Glos. d. ?
1893/94 13 apps 0 gls
1895/96 13 apps 0 gls
TOTAL 26 apps 0 gls
Club Record: Gloucester, Gloucester YMCA +.
Note: Club Captain 1895-96. Played for Gloucester 1891/92, 1892/93.

SEARLES, H.E (IF)
1913/14 2 apps 0 gls
TOTAL 2 apps 0 gls

SESSIONS, Walter (HB)
b. Qu4 1870 Gloucester d. ?
1893/94 2 apps 0 gls
TOTAL 2 apps 0 gls
Club Record: Gloucester, Cardiff +.
Note: Club Captain 1890-92. Brother of Wilfred Sessions. Played for Gloucester 1889/90, 1890/91, 1891/92, 1892/93.

SESSIONS, Wilfred (F)
b. 1869 Gloucester d. ?
1893/94 1 app 0 gls
TOTAL 1 app 0 gls
Note: Brother of Walter Sessions. Played for Gloucester 1889/90, 1890/91, 1891/92, 1892/93.

SHADGETT, J.B (CH)
b. Qu1 1889 Gloucester d. ?
1913/14 8 apps 1 gl
TOTAL 8 apps 1 gl

SHAW, W (IF)
1899/00 10 apps 17 gls
1900/01 9 apps 8 gls
TOTAL 19 apps 25 gls

SHERWOOD, Henry G (IF)
b. 1872 Stepney, London d. ?
1893/94 14 apps 4 gls
1894/95 15 apps 8 gls
1895/96 9 apps 3 gls
1897/98 4 apps 5 gls
1898/99 12 apps 9 gls
1899/00 2 app 4 gls
TOTAL 56 apps 33 gls
Note: Joint Club Secretary 1902-03. Played for Gloucester 1891/92, 1892/93.

SIDES, C (CH)
1913/14 2 apps 0 gls
TOTAL 2 apps 0 gls

SIMPSON, E (W)
1908/09 8 apps 2 gls
TOTAL 8 apps 2 gls

SLY, Ron Roger (HB)
b. 1877 Calstock, Cornwall d. ?
1898/99 6 apps 0 gls
1899/00 18 apps 2 gls
1902/03 7 apps 1 gl
1903/04 4 apps 0 gls
TOTAL 35 apps 3 gls

SMITH, A.H (HB)
1906/07 13 apps 0 gls
1907/08 12 apps 2 gls
1908/09 14 apps 0 gls
1909/10 11 apps 2 gls
TOTAL 50 apps 4 gls

SMITH, F.E (IF)
b. c 1881 d. ?
1900/01 1 app 0 gls
TOTAL 1 app 0 gls

SMITH, Harry (IF)
1906/07 9 apps 3 gls
TOTAL 9 apps 3 gls
Note: Played for Gloucester City 1907/08.

SMITH, Wilfred (W)
1906/07 11 apps 2 gls
1908/09 11 apps 8 gls
1909/10 15 apps 5 gls
TOTAL 37 apps 15 gls
Club Record: Gloucester City, Cheltenham Town +.
Note: Played for Gloucester City 1903/04, 1907/08.

SNELL, E.S (IF)
1894/95 2 apps 1 gl
1895/96 1 app 0 gls
TOTAL 3 apps 1 gl
Note: Played for Gloucester 1893/94.

SOMERVILLE, J.L (FB)
1893/94 14 apps 1 gl
TOTAL 14 apps 1 gl
Note: Club Captain 1892-93. Played for Gloucester 1891/92, 1892/93.

SPECK, George (GK)
b. Qu2 1862 Gloucester d. ?
1894/95 16 apps 0 gls
1895/96 16 apps 0 gls
1897/98 6 apps 0 gls
1898/99 11 apps 0 gls
TOTAL 49 apps 0 gls
Club Record: Nelson Villa, Gloucester, Warmley, Bristol City (0), Gloucester, Gloucester United +
Note: Brother of John Speck and Walter Speck. Played for Gloucester 1890/91, 1891/92, 1892/93.

SPENCE, Arthur (HB)
b. 1868 Frampton Cotterell, GLS d. ?
1895/96 13 apps 0 gls
TOTAL 13 apps 0 gls

SQUIER, Norman (CF)
b. Qu2 1888 Bulvan, Essex d. ?
1906/07 9 apps 11 gls
1907/08 12 apps 16 gls
1908/09 6 apps 5 gls
1909/10 2 apps 3 gls
TOTAL 29 apps 35 gls
Club Record: Chelmsford Town, Gloucester City +.

STAFFORD, ? (GK)
1900/01 1 app 0 gls
TOTAL 1 app 0 gls

STEBBING, E.F (IF)
1893/94 4 apps 2 gls
TOTAL 4 apps 2 gls
Note: Played for Gloucester 1890/91, 1891/92.

STEPHENS, A.J (IF)
1897/98 2 apps 1 gl
TOTAL 2 apps 1 gl
Note: Played for Gloucester 1896/97.

STOCK, J.W (W)
1898/99 1 app 0 gls
1899/00 7 apps 1 gl
TOTAL 8 apps 1 gl
Club Record: Saint Michael's, Gloucester +.

STOUT, Frank Moxon (HB)
b. 21/02/1877 Gloucester d. 30/05/1926 Storrington, Sussex
1893/94 11 apps 1 gl
1894/95 13 apps 0 gls
TOTAL 24 apps 1 gl
Note: Frank Stout also played rugby for Gloucester RFC and represented England 7 times. Brother of Percy Stout. Played for Gloucester 1891/92, 1892/93.

STOUT, Percy Wyford (F)
b. 20/11/1875 Gloucester d. 09/10/1937 Marylebone, London
1893/94 14 apps 8 gls
1894/95 13 apps 18 gls
TOTAL 27 apps 26 gls
Club Record: Gloucester, Wotton-under-Edge, Clifton, Bristol City (0) +.
Note: Percy Stout also played rugby for Gloucester RFC and represented England 5 times. Brother of Frank Stout. Played for Gloucester 1891/92, 1892/93.

TADMAN, Edgar Thomas Stuart (FB)
b. Qu3 Maidstone, Kent d. ?
1893-94 3 apps 0 gls
1894/95 11 apps 0 gls
1895/96 11 apps 0 gls
TOTAL 25 apps 0 gls
Note: Club Captain 1894-95.

TAYLOR, F.E (FB)
1906/07 2 apps 0 gls
1908/09 1 app 0 gls
1909/10 3 apps 0 gls
TOTAL 6 apps 0 gls

TRUEMAN, ? (FB)
1909/10 1 app 0 gls
TOTAL 1 app 0 gls

TRUEMAN, T (IF)
1903/04 5 apps 1 gl
TOTAL 5 apps 1 gl

TURNER, E.L (IF)
1894/95 1 app 0 gls
TOTAL 1 app 0 gls

TURNER, Ronald (CF)
b. 19/06/1885 Gillingham, Kent d. 15/08/1915 Suvla Bay, Gallipoli Peninsula, Turkey
1907/08 5 apps 17 gls
TOTAL 5 apps 17 gls
Club Record: Millwall, Cambridge University, Gloucester City +.
Note: Ronald Turner also played cricket for Gloucestershire. Killed in action WW1.

VAUGHAN, Charles Gilbert (FB)
b. 02/09/1868 Hewelsfield, Glos. d. 08/05/1952 McCammon, Idaho, USA
1894/95 3 apps 0 gls
TOTAL 3 apps 0 gls

VICKERY, Thomas T (HB)
b. 1892 Gloucester d. ?
1909/10 2 apps 0 gls
TOTAL 2 apps 0 gls
Note: Brother of William Vickery.

VICKERY, William C (GK)
b. 1887 Gloucester d. ?
1907/08 9 apps 0 gls
1908/09 14 apps 0 gls
1909/10 17 apps 0 gls
TOTAL 40 apps 0 gls
Note: Brother of Thomas Vickery. Club Captain 1908-10.

VINSON, George Alfred (HB)
b. Qu3 1885 Gloucester d. ?
1906/07 13 apps 0 gls
1907/08 14 apps 1 gl
1908/09 14 apps 0 gls
1909/10 17 apps 0 gls
TOTAL 58 apps 1 gl
Club Record: Gloucester City, Cheltenham Town +.
Note: Brother of William Vinson.

VINSON, William Druce (FB)
b. Qu2 1882 Gloucester d. ?
1902/03 3 apps 0 gls
1906/07 4 apps 0 gls
1907/08 1 app 0 gls
1908/09 13 apps 0 gls
TOTAL 21 apps 0 gls
Club Record: Saint Michael's, Gloucester City, Saint Michael's +.
Note: Brother of George Vinson.

WADE-SMITH, Rev. M (CH)
1894/95 12 apps 0 gls
1895/96 8 apps 0 gls
TOTAL 20 apps 0 gls
Club Record: Gloucester, Clifton Athletic +.

WAKEFIELD, J (CF)
1899/00 6 apps 1 gl
1900/01 10 apps 5 gls
1902/03 3 apps 0 gls
1903/04 10 apps 3 gls
TOTAL 29 apps 9 gls

WARD, ? (WH)
1893/94 1 app 0 gls
TOTAL 1 app 0 gls

WASHBOURN, James Gilbert (FB)
b. Qu4 1879 Hucclecote, Gloucester d. ?
1897/98 1 app 0 gls
1900/01 1 app 0 gls
TOTAL 2 apps 0 gls
Note: Played for Gloucester 1896/97.

WATTS, A (IF)
1908/09 13 apps 7 gls
1909/10 15 apps 2 gls
TOTAL 28 apps 9 gls

WHITE, C.F (HB)
1895/96 1 app 0 gls
TOTAL 1 app 0 gls
Note: Played for Gloucester 1892/93.

WILLETTS, W (GK)
1900/01 14 apps 0 gls
1902/03 7 apps 0 gls
1903/04 3 apps 0 gls
1906/07 14 apps 0 gls
TOTAL 38 apps 0 gls
Club Record: Gloucester, Saint Michael's, Gloucester City +.

WILLIAMS, ? (WH)
1909/10 1 app 0 gls
TOTAL 1 app 0 gls
Note: Scored 1 goal in his only league match but was disallowed by a disciplinary committee together with 2 points deducted from the club.

WILSON, C (W)
1900/01 10 apps 2 gls
TOTAL 10 apps 2 gls

CONTENDERS FOR A 'HALL OF FAME'

Frank Fielding, Arthur Fielding, George Speck, Henry Arkell

Percy Stout, Frank Stout, Henry Sherwood

HONOURS 1883-1914

1892-1893 Gloucestershire FA Senior Cup Runners-up
1894-1895 Gloucestershire FA Senior Cup Runners-up
1897-1898 Gloucester & District League – First Division Champions
1898-1899 Gloucester & District League – First Division Runners-up
　　　　　　 Mid Gloucestershire League Champions
1899-1900 Gloucester & District League – First Division Champions
　　　　　　 Mid Gloucestershire League Champions
1900-1901 Mid Gloucestershire League Champions
1902-1903 Gloucestershire FA Junior Cup Winners
1903-1904 Gloucester & District League – First Division Champions
1906-1907 Gloucester & District League – First Division Runners-up
　　　　　　 Cheltenham & District League – First Division Champions
　　　　　　 Gloucestershire FA Junior Cup Runners-up
1907-1908 North Gloucestershire League – First Division Champions
1908-1909 North Gloucestershire League – First Division Champions

MANAGERS 1883-1914

The precise definition of 'manager' is at times an arbitrary one, particularly in the pre-1915 years. This means that 'secretaries' in the early years who did not have managerial responsibilities but had overall responsibility of the club are mentioned.

W.H. Clarke 1883 - ? Secretary
A.S. King 1889 – 1890 Secretary
William H. Benfield 1890 – 1897? Secretary
James G. Washbourn 1897-1898 Secretary
Lionel A. Lane 1898-1899 Secretary
Randolph Lewis 1899-1902 Secretary
Henry W. Arkell/Henry G. Sherwood 1902 – 1904 Joint Secretaries
Frank R. Crawley 1903-1905 Secretary
J.E. Palmer 1906 – 1909 Secretary
Olly J.A. Carter 1909 – 1910 Secretary
A.J. Hayward 1910-1911 Secretary
H. Barry 1911-1914 Secretary

CLUB CAPTAINS 1889-1914

Charles F. Poole 1889-1890
Walter Sessions 1890-1892
J.L. Somerville 1892-1893
Frank B. Fielding 1893-1894
Edgar T.S. Tadman 1894-1895
Herbert H. Scott 1895-1896
W.H. Godby 1896-1897
Arthur F. Fielding 1897-1900
Frederick T. Rust 1900-1904
Ernest F. Davy 1906-1908
William C. Vickery 1908-1910
Charles A. Bretherton 1913-1914

RECORD OF ALL GAMES PER SEASON

Season		P	W	D	L		P	W	D	L		P	W	D	L	NOTE
1883-1884																No record
1884-1885							1					1				Only 1 match known
1885-1886							2	1	0	1		2	1	0	1	Only 2 matches known
1886 to 1889																Disbanded
1889-1890						OTHERS	18	6	2	10	TOTAL	18	6	2	10	2 games missing
1890-1891							20	13	0	7		20	13	0	7	
1891-1892							11	3	2	6		11	3	2	6	4 games missing
1892-1893							21	15	2	4		21	15	2	4	
1893-1894	LEAGUE	18	6	1	11		9	7	0	2		27	13	1	13	
1894-1895		22	10	4	8		5	3	0	2		27	13	4	10	
1895-1896		18	6	2	10		6	4	0	2		24	10	2	12	
1896-1897		-	-	-	-		12	3	1	8		12	3	1	8	1 game and 3 results missing
1897-1898		10	8	1	1		7	7	1	0		17	14	2	1	2 results missing
1898-1899		24	14	6	4		5	4	0	1		29	18	6	5	
1899-1900		28	25	3	0		5	1	1	3		33	26	4	3	
1900-1901		29	20	1	8		3	2	0	1		32	23	1	8	
1901 to 1902																Disbanded
1902-1903		8	1	4	3		14	11	2	1		22	12	6	4	
1903-1904		12	9	1	2		5	3	0	2		17	12	1	4	
1904 to 1906																Disbanded
1906-1907		22	18	2	2		14	8	1	5		36	26	3	7	
1907-1908		14	12	1	1		11	2	2	7		25	14	3	8	
1908-1909		14	11	3	0		12	2	3	7		26	13	6	7	1 game missing
1909-1910		28	8	12	8		8	3	1	4		36	11	13	12	1 result missing
1910 to 1913																YMCA in Gloucester Thursday League
1913-1914		11	1	3	7		6	1	2	3		17	2	5	9	YMCA Club 4 results missing

GROUNDS
1883-1895 Budding's Field
1895-1896 Avenue Road Ground (Tuffley Avenue)
1896-1897 Co-operative Field, India Road, Tredworth
1897-1898 Budding's Field
1898-1901 Avenue Road Ground (Tuffley Avenue)
1902-1910 Budding's Field
1910-1914 Llanthony, Hempsted

Also used Kingsholm on occasions between 1883 and 1900.

KIT COLOURS
Upto 1905 Black Shirts, with White Sleeves and Neckband, Black Shorts
1906 to 1908 Red and White Stripes, White Shorts
1909 to 1910 Black Shirts, with White Sleeves and Neckband, Black Shorts
1910 to 1913 Amber and Black Shirts
1913 to 1914 White Shirts

RECORDS IN LEAGUE MATCHES ONLY
Note: Unfortunately because of lack of information, these records are based on known facts only.

INDIVIDUALS 1893-1914

Most League Appearances
82 AF Fielding 1893-1904
58 GA Vinson 1906-1910
56 HG Sherwood 1893-1900
53 FB Fielding 1893-1899
50 HT Porter 1895-1901
50 AH Smith 1906-1910
49 G Speck 1894-1899
47 HW Arkell 1897-1904
47 AE Kent 1906-1910
45 FT Rust 1898-1904
43 FE Quixley 1906-1910
40 WC Vickery 1907-1910
38 W Willetts 1900-1907
37 AC Cragg 1893-1896
37 W Smith 1906-1910
35 RR Sly 1898-1904

Most League Goals
38 FB Fielding 1893-1899
37 FT Rust 1898-1904
35 N Squier 1906-1910
33 HG Sherwood 1893-1900
31 HT Porter 1895-1901
26 PW Stout 1893-1895
25 W Shaw 1899-1901
24 WA Jarman 1908-1910
22 AF Fielding 1893-1904
17 R Turner 1907-1908
15 AJ Carter 1906-1910
15 W Smith 1906-1910
12 AE Kent 1906-1910
10 A Parker 1902-1904

Highest League Scorer In A Season: 18, PW Stout, Bristol & Western District League, 1894-1895
Most Goals In One League Match: 5, PW Stout v Clevedon (H), 3 November 1894, Bristol & District League
5, W Shaw v Forest Green Rovers (H), 13 January 1900, Mid Gloucestershire League
5, FT Rust v Midland & South Western Junction Railway (A), 24 October 1903, Gloucester & District League
5, R Turner v Stroud (H), 23 November 1907, North Gloucestershire League
5, R Turner v Linden Old Boys (H), 30 November 1907, North Gloucestershire League
4, FB Fielding v Mangotsfield (H), 17 February 1894, Bristol & District League
4, PW Stout v Eastville Rovers (A), 16 March 1895, Bristol & District League
4, W Mason v Chalford (H), 6 April 1901, Mid Gloucestershire League
4, AE Bland v Winchcombe Town (H), 29 December 1906, Cheltenham & District League
4, R Turner v Stroud (A), 26 October 1907, North Gloucestershire League
4, N Squier v Stroud (H), 23 November 1907, North Gloucestershire League
4, N Squier v Linden Old Boys (H), 30 November 1907, North Gloucestershire League

TEAM 1893-1914

Record League Victory: 10-0 v Clevedon, 3 November 1894, Bristol & District League
                             10-0 v Forest Green Rovers, 13 January 1900, Mid Gloucestershire League
                             10-0 v Stroud, 23 November 1907, North Gloucestershire League
Record League Defeat: 1-8 v Trowbridge Town, 19 October 1895, Western League
Most League Points: 25, 1907-1908, North Gloucestershire League
Least League Points: 6, 1902-1903, Gloucester & District League
Most League Goals: 64, 1894-1895, Bristol & District League
Least League Goals: 10, 1901-1902, Gloucester & District League
Longest Sequence Of League Wins: 9, 18 March 1899 to 25 November 1899
Longest Sequence Of League Defeats: 5, 16 December 1893 to 10 February 1894
Longest Sequence Of Unbeaten League Matches: 24, 15 February 1908 to 16 October 1909
Longest Sequence Without A League Win: 12, 13 March 1910 to 21 February 1914
Successive Scoring Runs: 19, 21 November 1908 to 8 January 1910
Successive Non-Scoring Runs: 4, 1 November 1913 to 20 December 1913
Record League Attendance: 700 v Eastville Rovers, 11 November 1893 (at Kingsholm)

RECORD AGAINST LEAGUE CLUBS 1893-1914

OPPONENT	P	W	D	L	F	A	W	D	L	F	A	PTS	NOTES
BEDMINSTER	6	2	1	0	8	2	1	1	1	7	6	8	1 unplayed (drawn)
BOURTON ROVERS	4	1	1	0	3	2	1	1	0	4	1	6	
BRIMSCOMBE	7	1	1	1	6	3	3	0	1	14	6	10	
CAVENDISH HOUSE	2	1	0	0	2	1	1	0	0	1	0	4	Play in Cheltenham
CHALFORD	6	3	0	0	22	1	3	0	0	9	0	12	
CHELTENHAM TOWN	22	7	2	2	25	17	6	1	4	24	16	29	
CHELTENHAM TRAINING COLLEGE	2	1	0	0	1	0	0	0	1	1	3	2	
CIRENCESTER TOWN	2	1	0	0	4	1	1	0	0	6	0	4	
CLEVEDON	4	2	0	0	12	1	1	0	1	5	3	6	
CLIFTON	6	2	0	1	7	5	1	0	2	11	12	6	
DURSLEY	2	1	0	0	6	0	1	0	0	4	1	4	
EASTVILLE ROVERS	6	1	0	2	6	5	2	0	1	8	9	6	Now known as Bristol Rovers
EBLEY	8	4	0	0	17	4	3	1	0	10	1	15	
EVESHAM UNITED	2	0	1	0	2	2	0	0	1	0	3	1	
FOREST GREEN ROVERS	4	2	0	0	15	0	1	0	1	7	5	6	
HEREFORD THISTLE	2	0	1	0	6	6	0	0	0	0	0	1	1 game missing
LEDBURY VICTORIA	3	1	0	0	6	0	1	1	0	2	1	5	1 unplayed
LINDEN OLD BOYS	2	1	0	0	10	1	1	0	0	4	0	4	Play in Hempsted
LONGHOPE UNITED	2	0	0	0	0	3	0	0	0	0	0	0	1 score unknown
MANGOTSFIELD	6	2	0	0	8	2	1	1	1	3	4	7	1 game missing
MIDLAND & SOUTH WESTERN JUNCTION RAILWAY	6	2	0	1	7	4	2	1	0	11	3	9	Play in Cirencester
MINSTERWORTH	2	0	0	1	0	5	0	0	1	0	2	0	
MITCHELDEAN	2	0	1	0	1	1	0	0	0	0	0	1	1 result unknown
NEWNHAM EXCELSIOR	2	1	0	0	2	0	0	0	1	0	2	2	
PRICE WALKERS	2	1	0	0	8	0	1	0	0	1	0	4	Play in Gloucester
ROSELEIGH	2	1	0	0	0	0	0	0	1	2	3	2	1 unplayed (won). Play in Cheltenham
ROSS KYRLE	6	1	1	1	8	4	3	0	0	8	1	9	
ROSS TOWN	10	3	2	0	14	5	2	1	2	10	7	13	
SAINT GEORGE	6	1	0	2	4	4	1	0	2	4	8	4	Play in Bristol
SAINT MICHAEL'S	2	0	0	1	3	4	0	0	1	0	1	0	Play in Hempsted
SAINT PAUL'S	2	0	1	0	3	3	0	0	0	0	0	1	1 game missing. Play in Bristol
SAINT PAUL'S UNITED	10	4	0	1	16	3	3	1	1	12	9	15	Play in Cheltenham
SHARPNESS	6	1	2	0	12	4	1	1	1	9	7	6	
STAPLE HILL	6	0	2	1	2	4	0	0	3	2	8	2	
STONEHOUSE	2	1	0	0	7	4	1	0	0	3	0	4	
STROUD	6	2	1	0	14	2	1	1	1	12	5	6	
SWINDON WANDERERS	4	1	1	0	2	0	0	0	1	2	3	3	1 game missing, 1 unplayed (drawn)
TEWKESBURY ABBEY	10	3	1	1	18	9	1	2	2	5	8	7	
TEWKESBURY TOWN	14	5	2	0	24	8	6	1	0	17	7	23	
TROWBRIDGE TOWN	6	0	0	3	4	14	1	0	2	7	11	0	
TUFFLEY & WHADDON	2	0	0	1	1	5	0	0	1	0	4	0	
WARMLEY	6	1	0	2	4	9	0	0	3	1	11	2	
WESTGATE	2	1	0	0	4	0	0	0	1	1	2	0	Play in Gloucester
WINCHCOMBE TOWN	4	2	0	0	9	2	0	2	0	2	2	6	
WOODCHESTER	2	1	0	0	2	0	1	0	0	2	1	4	

LIST OF OTHER GAMES 1884-1914

1884/1885 v EASTVILLE ROVERS (?) Result unknown

02/01/1886 v EASTVILLE ROVERS (A) Lost 0-1

00/00/1886 v Unknown opponent (H) Won (There was a mention of a Junior Cup match following the Eastville Rovers friendly match)

05/10/1889 v CLIFTON (A) Lost 0-6
R Murch; A Gardner, AE Johnson; WAS Ely, Walter Sessions, HJ Chadborn; Rev. RD Wade, AS King, CN Chadborn, CF Poole, FB Fielding.

19/10/1889 v HEREFORD TOWN (A) Lost 1-8
GR Bonnor; AE Johnson, HF Grimley; AG Taynton, FB Fielding, LH Carter; JH Blake, Walter Sessions, CN Chadborn, AS King, CF Poole.
Scorer: Taynton.

26/10/1889 v CLIFTON RESERVES (H) Won 10-0 (Gloucestershire Junior Challenge Cup 1st Round)
AB Cooke; Rev. H.L. Brereton, GR Bonnor; WAS Ely, HF Grimley, Walter Sessions; Rev. RD Wade, GB Perkins, HV Hockin, CF Poole, FB Fielding.
Scorers: Perkins (2), Wade (4), Hockin, Grimley, ?. (2 goals missing).

02/11/1889 v CLIFTON (H) Lost 3-5
AB Cooke; A Gardner, S Higginson; WAS Ely, HF Grimley, W Munro; Rev. RD Wade, GB Perkins, CM Henderson, HV Hockin, CF Poole.
Scorers: Henderson, Poole (pen), Wade.

09/11/1889 v OLD BOYS QUEEN ELIZABETH HOSPITAL BRISTOL (H) Won 8-1 (Gloucestershire Junior Challenge Cup 2nd Round)
AB Cooke; Rev. HL Brereton, A Gardner; WH Vickery, S Higginson, AE Johnson; HJ Chadborn, Rev. RD Wade, CM Henderson, CF Poole, FB Fielding.
Scorers: Henderson (4), Poole (3), Fielding.

16/11/1889 v SWINDON TOWN (A) Lost 0-10
AB Cooke; O Drewett, W Hare; S Higginson, WH Vickery, GP Davies; HJ Chadborn, AS King, Rev. RD Wade, AG Taynton, FB Fielding.

23/11/1889 v WARMLEY RESERVES (A) Lost 2-3 (Gloucestershire Junior Challenge Cup Semi-Final)
AB Cooke; A Gardner, GR Bonnor; S Higginson, WH Vickery, AB Macfarlane; GB Perkins, Rev. RD Wade, CM Henderson, CF Poole, FB Fielding.
Scorers: Wade, Fielding.

30/11/1889 v TEWKESBURY (A) Lost 1-9
AB Cooke; AB Macfarlane, O Drewett; AE Johnson, NF Wheaton, HJ Chadborn; GB Perkins, Rev. RD Wade, TB Powell, AS King, FB Fielding.
Scorer: Wade.

14/12/1889 v WORCESTER ROVERS (A) Lost 1-7
E Platt; FM Morris, FJ Platt; WAS Ely, H Barnard, F Fletcher; PE Creese, Rev. RD Wade, Walter Sessions, AS King, FB Fielding.
Scorer: ?. (1 goal missing).

21/12/1889 v NELSON VILLA (H) Won 11-2
(No match report in The Citizen)
Scorers: ?. (11 goals missing).
The team were called a Gloucester XI.

26/12/1889 v CHELTENHAM (H) Won 7-0
(No match report in The Citizen)
Scorers: ?. (7 goals missing).

28/12/1889 v CLIFTON (H) Won 3-2
AB Cooke; FJ Platt, W Cooper; S Ward, LH Carter, Wilfred Sessions; TB Powell, FB Fielding, Walter Sessions, Rev. RD Wade, GB Perkins.
Scorers: Fielding, Powell (2).

25/01/1890 v HEREFORD TOWN (H) Lost 2-3
AB Cooke; AB Macfarlane, LH Carter; GJ Ward, Walter Sessions; PE Creese, Rev. RD Wade, CM Henderson, CF Poole, FB Fielding (only ten players used).
Scorers: ?. (2 goals missing).

01/02/1890 v SWINDON TOWN (H) Won 3-2
G Speck; FJ Platt, AB Macfarlane; WAS Ely, LH Carter, Walter Sessions; Rev. RD Wade, GB Perkins, HV Hockin, CF Poole, FB Fielding.
Scorers: Wade, Hockin, Poole.

THE CITIZEN FOR FEBRUARY MISSING AT THE RECORD OFFICE

01/03/1890 v GLOUCESTER COUNTY SCHOOL (H) Lost 1-4
(No match report in The Citizen)
Scorer: ?. (1 goal missing).

15/03/1890 v WORCESTER ROVERS (H) Drew 2-2
E Platt; Rev. HL Brereton, FJ Platt; F Fletcher, HV Hockin, Walter Sessions; S Higginson, Rev. RD Wade, CM Henderson, CF Poole, FB Fielding.
Scorer: Poole (2).

22/03/1890 v CARDIFF (A) Drew 1-1
E Platt; FJ Platt, AN Other; WAS Ely, W Speck, Walter Sesions; TB Powell, Rev. RD Wade, CM Henderson, CF Poole, FB Fielding.
Scorer: Ely.

29/03/1890 v LEDBURY (A) Lost 3-4
FW Grimshaw; A Pink, Walter Sessions; GP Davies, LH Carter, F Fletcher; W Speck, Rev. RD Wade, CF Poole, AS King, FB Fielding.
Scorers: ?. (3 goals missing)

1889/1890 v WARMLEY (H) missing

1889/1890 v WARMLEY (A) missing

04/10/1890 v XIII COLTS (H) Won 4-3
WL Buchanan; AB Macfarlane, A Gardner; Walter Sessions, F Fletcher, J King; GB Perkins, Rev. RD Wade, CM Henderson, CF Poole, FB Fielding.
Scorers: Henderson (3), Fielding.

11/10/1890 v EVESHAM (A) Won 9-0
G Speck; AB Macfarlane, T Prince; J Rodwell, WAS Ely, AE Johnson; Rev. RD Wade, GB Perkins, CM Henderson, CF Poole, FB Fielding.
Scorers: Perkins (2), Henderson (2), Fielding (2), Wade (2), Macfarlane.

18/10/1890 v CLIFTON (H) Won 4-2
G Speck; AB Macfarlane, T Prince; J King, HV Hockin, J Rodwell; GB Perkins, Rev. RD Wade, CM Henderson,
CF Poole, FB Fielding.
Scorers: Henderson (2), Wade, King.

25/10/1890 v DEAN CLOSE SCHOOL (H) Won 7-1
T Casswell; AB Macfarlane, L Greaves; WAS Ely, HV Hockin, GR Phillips; GB Perkins, Rev. RD Wade, CM Henderson, FB Fielding, J King.
Scorers: Henderson (6), King.

01/11/1890 v WORCESTER ROVERS (A) Lost 2-5
W Jones; L Greaves, T Prince; WAS Ely, GR Phillips, GP Davies; S Higginson, Rev. RD Wade, FB Fielding, WG Matthews, EF Stebbing.
Scorers: Matthews, Higginson.

08/11/1890 v TEWKESBURY (H) Won 7-0
G Speck; L Greaves, T Prince; WAS Ely, J King, GR Phillips; S Higginson, Rev. RD Wade, CM Henderson, FB Fielding, Rev. AM Bolland.
Scorers: Henderson (4), Higginson (2), Fielding.

15/11/1890 v CARDIFF (H) Won 6-3
G Speck; AB Macfarlane, T Prince; J King, WAS Ely, GR Phillips; S Higginson, Rev. RD Wade, CM Henderson, FB Fielding, CF Poole.
Scorers: Higginson, Poole (3), Wade, Henderson.

22/11/1890 v GLOUCESTER COUNTY SCHOOLS (H) Lost 4-5
G Speck; AB Macfarlane, AN Other; Walter Sessions, WAS Ely, PW Poole; S Higginson, Rev. RD Wade, GB Perkins, CF Poole, FB Fielding.
Scorers: Fielding (2), CF Poole (2).

29/11/1890 v HEREFORD (A) Lost 3-4
G Speck; GR Phillips, T Prince; Walter Sessions, HV Hockin, WAS Ely; S Higginson, Rev. RD Wade, CM Henderson, CF Poole, FB Fielding.
Scorers: Henderson (2), Wade.

06/12/1890 v BRISTOL SAINT GEORGE'S (A) Lost 2-5
G Speck; GR Phillips, T Prince; Walter Sessions, J King, WAS Ely; GB Perkins, Rev. RD Wade, CM Henderson, CF Poole, FB Fielding.
Scorers: Sessions (2).

13/12/1890 v GLOUCESTER COUNTY SCHOOLS (A) Lost 2-4 (Game was scratched due to frost but played a game on the longer grass)
G Speck; GR Phillip, T Prince; WAS Ely, Walter Sessions, H Barnard; S Higginson, Rev. RD Wade, CF Poole, WG Matthews, FB Fielding.
Scorers: ?. (2 goals missing).

10/01/1891 v LEDBURY (A) postponed
Game was postponed due to bad weather. In fact Gloucester remained idle for about 6 weeks. The following team was selected:
G Speck; AB Macfarlane, GR Phillips; Walter Sessions, F Fletcher, AE Johnson; GB Perkins, Rev. RD Wade, JOT Powell, WG Matthews, FB Fielding.

15/01/1891 v TEWKESBURY (A) postponed

24/01/1891 v GLOUCESTER COUNTY SCHOOLS (A) Won 5-4
G Speck; AB Macfarlane, T Prince; Walter Sessions, WAS Ely, Wilfred Sessions; GB Perkins, Rev. RD Wade, R Clemenson, WG Matthews, FB Fielding.
Scorers: Wade, Clemenson (2), Ely, Fielding.

31/01/1891 v GLOUCESTER COUNTY SCHOOLS (H) Won 3-1 (Gloucester were due to play Malvern Link this day but they were unable to fulfil fixture so Gloucester County Schools replaced them).
G Speck; AB Macfarlane, T Prince; WAS Ely, FC Saunders, Walter Sessions; GB Perkins, Rev. RD Wade, R Clemenson, ? Oakley, FB Fielding.
Scorers: ?. (3 goals missing).

07/02/1891 v NELSON VILLA (H) Won 6-1
G Speck; AB Macfarlane, Walter Sessions; J King, FC Saunders, C Mitchell; MB Lewis, Rev. RD Wade, CM Henderson, R Clemenson, FB Fielding.
Scorers: Henderson (3), Sessions, Fielding, Clemenson.

14/02/1891 v WORCESTER ROVERS (H) Won 7-2
G Speck; AB Macfarlane, A Bevan; Walter Sessions, EJD Mitchell, J King; MB Lewis, Rev. RD Wade, CM Henderson, CF Poole, FB Fielding.
Scorers: Henderson (5), Fielding (2).

21/02/1891 v DEAN CLOSE SCHOOL (A) Lost 0-2
G Speck; AB Macfarlane, JL Somerville; Walter Sessions, GR Phillips, J King; WG Matthews, Rev. RD Wade, CM Henderson, CF Poole, FB Fielding.

28/02/1891 v HEREFORD (H) Lost 0-4
G Speck; A Bevan, Walter Sessions; HV Hockin, EJD Mitchell, J King; WG Matthews, Rev. RD Wade, CM Henderson, CF Poole, FB Fielding.

07/03/1891 v CIRENCESTER (H) Won 4-1
G Speck; AB Macfarlane, A Bevan; EJD Mitchell, GR Phillips, ? Walters; J King, WG Matthews, CM Henderson, Walter Sessions, FB Fielding.
Scorers: ?. (4 goals missing).

14/03/1891 v NELSON VILLA (H) Won 4-0 (Gloucester were due to play Ledbury this day but they were unable to keep engagement so Nelson Villa replaced them).
(No match report in The Citizen)
Scorers: ?. (4 goals missing).

21/03/1891 v BRISTOL SAINT GEORGE'S (H) Won 3-2
J Speck; AB Macfarlane, A Bevan; Walter Sessions, GR Phillips, J King; G Speck, CM Henderson, CF Palmer, WG Matthews, FB Fielding.
Scorers: Palmer (2), Matthews.
The team was photographed prior to the game

26/09/1891 v CRYPT GRAMMAR SCHOOL (A) Lost 1-2
(Not officially a Gloucester game but they played under that name. No match report in The Citizen)
Scorer: ?. (1 goal missing).

10/10/1891 v SWINDON TOWN (A) Match abandoned

17/10/1891 v UNITED SCHOOLS OF GLOUCESTER (H) Won 7-2
G Speck; AB Macfarlane, FH Green; A Poole, Walter Sessions, Rev. JH Harvey; GB Perkins, J Brazier,
Rev. AM Bolland, A Wright, R Bagley.
Scorers: Bolland (3), Bagley, Wright, ?. (2 goals missing).

07/11/1891 v CIRENCESTER (A) Drew 1-1
G Speck; AB Macfarlane, JL Somerville; WH Benfield, Walter Sessions, FM Stout; GB Perkins, J Brazier,
Rev. AM Bolland, R Bagley, PW Stout.
Scorer: Sessions.

14/11/1891 v LEDBURY (H) Won 4-0
G Speck; JL Somerville, AB Macfarlane; HH Scott, Walter Sessions, FM Stout; GB Perkins, J Brazier,
CM Henderson, R Bagley, PW Stout.
Scorers: Henderson (4).

21/11/1891 v MALVERN (A) Scratched. Malvern engaged in a cup tie.

28/11/1891 v SWINDON Y.M.F.A. (H) Lost 2-4
G Speck; JL Somerville, HH Scott; H Benfield, Walter Sessions, AA Matthews; HT Robins, GB Perkins,
CM Henderson, EF Stebbing, PW Stout.
Scorers: ?. (2 goals missing).

05/12/1891 v HEREFORD (H, Crypt School Ground, Friars' Orchard)) Lost 3-4
G Speck; JL Somerville, HH Scott; WH Benfield, AA Matthews, Walter Sessions; GB Perkins, AS King,
A Poole,
J Brazier, EF Stebbing.
Scorers: Poole, ?. (2 goals missing).

19/12/1891 v BRISTOL SAINT GEORGE'S (A) Won 1-0   Att: 5,000
G Speck; JL Somerville, HH Scott; AE Johnson, Walter Sessions, AN Other; J Brazier, HT Robins,
CM Henderson, EF Stebbing, PW Stout.
Scorer: Stebbing.

26/12/1891 v CLIFTON (H) Abandoned as Clifton unable to raise a team
G Speck; FM Morris, HH Scott; AA Matthews, Walter Sessions, AE Johnson; HT Robins, Rev. AM Bolland,
Wilfred Sessions, FB Fielding, PW Stout.
(The above team was selected for this game)

28/12/1891 v WILFRED SESSIONS HOLIDAY TEAM (H) Won 4-3
(Presumably most of the players that were selected for the Clifton game participated)

16/01/1892 v WORCESTER ROVERS (A) ?
J Speck; JL Somerville, FM Morris; WH Benfield, J King, Walter Sessions; A Jones, HT Robins,
Rev. AM Bolland, PW Stout, EF Stebbing.
Scorers: ?.

23/01/1892 v DEAN CLOSE SCHOOL (A) ?
G Speck; JL Somerville, HH Scott; F Walker, Walter Sessions, WH Benfield; PW Stout, EF Stebbing,
Rev. AM Bolland, AN Other, HG Sherwood.
Scorers: ?.

30/01/1892 v BRISTOL SAINT GEORGE'S (H) Lost 3-4 (Gloucestershire Senior Cup 1st Round)
G Speck; HH Scott, TG Sampson; AE Johnson, Walter Sessions, AA Matthews; GB Perkins, HT Robins, JOT Powell, PW Stout, HG Sherwood.
Scorers: Robins, Perkins, Powell.

06/02/1892 v STROUD CASUALS (A) Drew 3-3
G Speck; TG Sampson, E Bates; HH Scott, Rev. JH Harvey, GH Woodward; PW Stout, HG Sherwood, JL Somerville, HT Robins, AN Other.
Scorers: Harvey (2), Sherwood.

20/02/1892 v CLIFTON (H) Match abandoned. Heavy snow.

27/02/1892 v LEDBURY (A) ?
G Speck; JL Somerville, E Bates; FM Morris, HH Scott, WH Benfield; HG Sherwood, PW Stout, JOT Powell, HT Robins, TB Powell.

05/03/1892 v SWINDON TOWN (A) Lost 0-6
(No match report in The Citizen).

19/03/1892 v BRISTOL SAINT GEORGE'S (A) Lost 1-3
G Speck; JL Somerville, E Bates; FM Morris, HH Scott, WH Benfield; HT Robins, GB Perkins, Rev. JH Harvey, PW Stout, HG Sherwood.
Scorer: ?. (1 goal missing).

08/10/1892 v DEAN CLOSE SCHOOL (A) Lost 1-3
G Speck; E Bates, JL Somerville; H Barnard, HH Scott, WH Benfield; WG Matthews, Rev. RD Wade, FB Fielding, PW Stout, HT Robins.
Scorer: ?. (1 goal missing)

15/10/1892 v SWINDON SAINT MARK'S (H) Won 4-1
RH Hornsby; RN Green, E Bates; Rev. JH Harvey, JL Somerville, HH Scott; WG Matthews, HT Robins, PW Stout, AN Other, FB Fielding.
Scorers: ?. (4 goals missing).

22/10/1892 v CIRENCESTER (A) Won 4-1
G Speck; RN Green, E Bates; HH Scott, JL Somerville, Rev. JH Harvey; PW Stout, WT Gardner, FB Fielding, WG Matthews, HT Robins.
Scorers: Fielding (2), Matthews (2).

29/10/1892 v TEWKESBURY (H) Won 5-0
? Darkin; JL Somerville, PA Vigne; FM Stout, HH Scott, GH Woodward; JM Crofts, HT Robins, WT Gardner, HG Sherwood, FB Fielding.
Scorers: Sherwood, Fielding, own goal, Crofts, ?. (1 goal missing).

05/11/1892 v ROSS (H) Won
G Speck; RN Green, E Bates; Rev. JH Harvey, HH Scott, GH Woodward; WG Matthews, HT Robins, A Forest, PW Stout, WT Gardner.
Scorers: ?.

12/11/1892 v CLIFTON (A) Drew 3-3
G Speck; RN Green, E Bates; Rev. JH Harvey, JL Somerville, HH Scott; WG Matthews, HT Robins, FB Fielding, PW Stout, WT Gardner.
Scorers: Robins, Gardner, Fielding.

19/11/1892 v WINCHCOMBE (A) Won 5-0
G Speck; E Bates, PA Vigne; GH Woodward, HH Scott, AN Other; WG Matthews, HT Robins, FB Fielding, PW Stout, WT Gardner.
Scorers: Gardner, Fielding, Robins, Stout, Scott.

26/11/1892 v EVESHAM (H) Won 6-1
G Speck; E Bates, AC Cragg; JL Somerville, HH Scott, FM Stout; HG Sherwood, HT Robins, FB Fielding, PW Stout, WT Gardner.
Scorers: Fielding (2), Somerville, Sherwood, Robins, PW Stout.

10/12/1892 v ROSS (H) Won 12-0
G Speck; E Bates, AC Cragg; HH Scott, JL Somerville, AN Other; HG Sherwood, HT Robins, FB Fielding, A Forest, WT Gardner.
Scorers: Fielding (5), Robins (3), Sherwood (3), Gardner.

17/12/1892 v BRISTOL SAINT GEORGE'S (H) Won 3-0
G Speck; AC Cragg, RN Green; Rev. JH Harvey, HH Scott, JL Somerville; WG Matthews, HT Robins, FB Fielding, PW Stout, WT Gardner.
Scorers: Fielding (2), Gardner.

24/12/1892 v STROUD CASUALS (H) Won 13-1
G Speck; AC Cragg, HH Scott; AE Johnson, CF White, Walter Sessions; HT Robins, A Forest, FB Fielding, JOT Powell, S McLinton.
Scorers: Sessions, Robins (2), Fielding (3), Powell (2), McLinton (5).

07/01/1893 v WINCHCOMBE (H) Postponed. Pitch unfit to play.

14/01/1893 v BRISTOL SAINT GEORGE'S (A) Drew 1-1
G Speck; AC Cragg, PA Vigne; Walter Sessions, CF White, HH Scott; PW Stout, WT Gardner, FB Fielding, C McLinton, HT Robins.
Scorer: Stout.

28/01/1893 v CLIFTON (A) Won 6-1 (Gloucestershire Senior Cup 1st Round)
G Speck; AC Cragg, RN Green; Rev. JH Harvey, HH Scott, AN Other; HT Robins, HG Sherwood, FB Fielding, HW Jones, WT Gardner.
Scorers: Sherwood (2), Fielding (3), ?. (1 goal missing).

04/02/1893 v DEAN CLOSE SCHOOL (H) Lost 1-2
G Speck; AC Cragg, AN Other; JL Somerville, HH Scott, AE Johnson; S Wood, HT Robins, FB Fielding, C McLinton, WT Gardner.
Scorer: ?. (1 goal missing).

11/02/1893 v LEDBURY (H) Lost 1-2
G Speck; RN Green, AC Cragg; AE Johnson, HH Scott, JL Somerville; S Wood, HT Robins, AN Other, WT Gardner, FB Fielding.
Scorer: ?. (1 goal missing).

18/02/1893 v ROSS (A) Won 8-0
RH Hornsby; JL Somerville, RS Penfold; AE Johnson, HH Scott, FM Stout; JM Crofts, HT Robins, FB Fielding, HW Jones, C McLinton.
Scorers: Fielding (4), Robins (3), Jones.

25/02/1893 v BEDMINSTER (H) Won 5-0 (Gloucestershire Senior Cup Semi-Final)   Att: 2,000
G Speck; AC Cragg, RN Green; Rev. JH Harvey, HH Scott, JL Somerville; HG Sherwood, HT Robins, Wilfred Sessions, PW Stout, FB Fielding.
Scorers: Fielding (2), Sessions (2), Robins.
Gate receipts = £20

04/03/1893 v EVESHAM (A) Won 3-2
G Speck; RN Green, JL Somerville; AE Johnson, HH Scott, Rev. JH Harvey; WG Matthews, HT Robins, A Forest, HW Jones, FB Fielding.
Scorers: Robins, Matthews, ?. (1 goal missing).

11/03/1893 v CIRENCESTER (H) Won 7-0
HH Scott, HT Robins, FB Fielding (only these three players mentioned in The Citizen).
Scorers: ?. (7 goals missing).

25/03/1893 v CLIFTON (H) Won 12-0
G Speck; HH Scott, WG Matthews, HG Sherwood, FB Fielding, HT Robins, HW Jones (only seven players mentioned in The Citizen).
Scorers: Sherwood (4), Fielding (3), Robins (3), Matthews, Jones.

01/04/1893 v WARMLEY (Bedminster) Lost 1-4 (Gloucestershire Senior Cup Final)   Att: 3,000-4,000
G Speck; AC Cragg, RN Green; JL Somerville, HH Scott, Rev. JH Harvey; FB Fielding, PW Stout, Wilfred Sessions, HG Sherwood, HT Robins.
Scorer: ?. (1 goal missing).

The earliest team photograph c1892-1893

v MANGOTSFIELD (H) Lost to frost

v MANGOTSFIELD (A) Lost to frost.

07/10/1893 v SWINDON TOWN ATHLETIC (H) Won 3-1
SJF Kent; RN Green, JL Somerville; Rev. JH Harvey, HH Scott, AC Cragg; WG Matthews, HT Robins, PW Stout, EF Stebbing, FB Fielding.
Scorers: Stout (2), Fielding.

21/10/1893 v CIRENCESTER (H) Won 8-1 (Cirencester Association Cup)
SJF Kent; JL Somerville, PA Vigne; T Clark, HH Scott, Walter Sessions; FB Fielding, AF Fielding, PW Stout, HT Robins, HG Sherwood.
Scorers: Sherwood (2), Stout (2), Robins, FB Fielding, AF Fielding, ?. (1 goal missing)
(Line-up and scorers courtesy of The Gloucester Standard & Gloucestershire News)

25/11/1893 v CIRENCESTER (H) Won 5-0
SJF Kent; JL Somerville, AC Cragg; FM Stout, HH Scott, T. Clark; HT Robins, WG Matthews, FB Fielding, EF Stebbing, PW Stout.
Scorers: ?. (5 goals missing).

09/12/1893 v DEAN CLOSE SCHOOL (A) Lost 1-2
(No match report in The Citizen)
Scorer: ?. (1 goal missing).

26/12/1893 v EVESHAM WANDERERS (A) Won 4-3
(Result from Gloucestershire Chronicle)
Scorers: ?. (4 goals missing)

27/01/1894 v CLIFTON (H) Won 8-0 (Gloucestershire Senior Cup)
SJF Kent; JL Somerville, CH Norrington; Walter Sessions, HH Scott, FM Stout; FB Fielding, PW Stout, Wilfred Sessions, AC Cragg, HG Sherwood.
Scorers: Sherwood, Wilfred Sessions (2), PW Stout (2), Walter Sessions (2), Fielding.

03/02/1894 v DEAN CLOSE SCHOOL (H) Won 13-2
SJF Kent; JL Somerville, CH Norrington; FM Stout, HH Scott, ETS Tadman; HG Sherwood, AC Cragg, FB Fielding, AF Fielding, PW Stout.
Scorers: Sherwood (4), FB Fielding (4), AF Fielding (2), Scott, FM Stout, Cragg.
(Line-up and scorers courtesy of The Gloucester Standard & Gloucestershire News)

24/02/1894 v EASTVILLE ROVERS (H) Lost 0-1 (Gloucestershire Senior Cup Semi-Final)   Att: 1,000
SJF Kent; JL Somerville, AC Cragg; Walter Sessions, HH Scott, FM Stout; HG Sherwood, AC Hoitt, FB Fielding, ES Snell, PW Stout.

10/03/1894 v MR J HANMAN'S XI (H) Won 6-1
FB Fielding. (Only this player mentioned in The Journal)
Scorers: Fielding (3), ?. (3 goals missing).

29/09/1894 v DEAN CLOSE SCHOOL (H) Won 5-3
G Speck; CG Vaughan, AC Cragg; HT Robins, WT Pitt, FM Stout; AF Fielding, HG Sherwood, PW Stout, FB Fielding, JE Turner.
Scorers: PW Stout, AF Fielding, Sherwood (2).

13/10/1894 v DEAN CLOSE SCHOOL (A) Lost 1-2
G Speck; CG Vaughan; WT Pitt, AC Cragg, Rev. M.Wade-Smith; AF Fielding, HG Sherwood, PW Stout, FB Fielding, HT Robins. (only ten players used).
Scorer; Sherwood.

26/01/1895 v SAINT PAUL'S (H) Won   (Gloucestershire Cup)
G Speck; RC Fowler, ETS Tadman; Rev. M Wade-Smith, ? Taylor, FM Stout; HG Sherwood, ES Snell, PW Stout,
AF Fielding, FB Fielding.
Scorers: ?.

23/02/1895 v MANGOTSFIELD (H) Won 4-2 (Gloucestershire Cup Semi-Final)
(No match report in The Citizen/Journal)
Scorers: ?. (4 goals missing).

14/04/1895 v SAINT GEORGE (N, Chequers) Lost 3-4 (Gloucestershire Cup Final)
G Speck; RC Fowler, ETS Tadman; AC Cragg, Rev. M Wade-Smith, FM Stout; HG Sherwood, JOT Powell, PW Stout, AF Fielding, FB Fielding.
Scorers: PW Stout (2), ?. (1 goal missing).

21/09/1895 v CHELTENHAM (H) Won 3-1
J Speck; AE Goodwin, HD Green; ETS Tadman, HH Scott, A Spence; HG Sherwood, GC Clutterbuck, FB Fielding, AF Fielding, AP Frith.
Scorers: AF Fielding, Clutterbuck, Sherwood.

12/10/1895 v BOURNEMOUTH (H) Conceded due to financial constraints (English Amateur Cup)

23/11/1895 v CARDIFF (H) Lost 0-2 (Originally a Western League match but Cardiff withdrew from the League)
G Speck; AC Cragg, ETS Tadman; HH Scott, Rev. M Wade-Smith, A Spence; AF Fielding, FB Fielding, H Harris, HG Sherwood, GC Clutterbuck.

26/12/1895 v BRISTOL SOUTH END (A) Lost 1-4
G Speck; AP Frith, FM Morris; CF White, HH Scott, A Spence; AF Fielding, FB Fielding, HG Sherwood, ET James, GC Clutterbuck.
Scorer; James.

27/12/1895 v BEDMINSTER (H) Won 2-1
G Speck; AP Frith, RC Fowler; CF White, HH Scott, A Spence; AF Fielding, FB Fielding, HG Sherwood, COH Sewell, GC Clutterbuck.
Scorers: FB Fielding, Sherwood.

28/12/1895 v CHELTENHAM (A) Won 5-0
G Speck; RC Fowler, AP Frith; FM Morris, HH Scott, A Spence; AF Fielding, FB Fielding, COH Sewell, ET James, HG Sherwood.
Scorers: FB Fielding, Sherwood, Sewell, Scott, AF Fielding.

1895/1896 v SOUTH END WEDNESDAY (?) Won 5-2
G Speck; GL Jessop, AP Frith; AC Cragg, RC Fowler, A Spence; HG Sherwood, ES Snell, EC Wright, AF Fielding, FB Fielding.
Scorers: Wright (2), FB Fielding (2), AF Fielding.
(Line-up courtesy of The Pink 'Un c1933)

10/10/1896 v TEWKESBURY ABBEY (H) Lost 0-2
HT Robins; WH Hicks, JG Washbourne; WH Godby, JA Oakey, WA Brown; EHP Scantlebury, J Radford, AJ Stephens, AH Robson, WA Harris.

17/10/1896 v ROSS TOWN (A) Lost 1-4
A Cowley; WH Hicks, A Flower; WH Godby, WA Brown, JG Washbourne; AJ Stephens, AH Robson, EHP Scantlebury, AF Fielding, AN Other.
Scorer: Stephens.

24/10/1896 v STROUD (A) Lost 1-2
(No mention of Gloucester players in The Citizen)
Scorer: ?.

31/10/1896 v WOTTON-UNDER-EDGE (H) Won 2-1
A Cowley; JG Washbourne, WH Hicks; EHP Scantlebury, JA Oakey, WA Brown; HW Arkell, AJ Stephens,
WH Godby, J Sabin, WA Harris.
Scorers: Sabin, Harris.

07/11/1896 v CHALFORD (H) Drew 1-1
A Cowley; JG Washbourne, WH Hicks; WH Godby, EHP Scantlebury, WA Brown; AH Robson, JC Hammond,
ET Talbot, HW Arkell, WA Harris.
Scorer: Arkell.

14/11/1896 v DEAN CLOSE SCHOOL (H) Won 2-1
A Cowley; JG Washbourne, WH Hicks; EHP Scantlebury, JA Oakey, WA Brown; AJ Stephens, AH Robson,
J Sabin, HW Arkell, WH Godby.
Scorer: Arkell (2).

21/11/1896 v WYCLIFFE COLLEGE (A) ?
A Cowley; JG Washbourne, WH Hicks; JC Hammond, EHP Scantlebury, WA Brown; MR Luckman,
HW Arkell, AJ Stephens, J Sabin, WA Harris.

05/12/1896 v CHELTENHAM (H) Won 2-0
A Cowley; JG Washbourne, WH Hicks; AC Cragg, EHP Scantlebury, WA Brown; AJ Stephens, WH Godby,
A Roberts, ET James, HW Arkell.
Scorers: Roberts, James.

12/12/1896 v PRICE WALKERS (H) Lost 0-1
A Cowley; JG Washbourne, WH Hicks; EHP Scantlebury, WT Pitt, WA Brown; AJ Stephens, WH Godby,
ET James, HW Arkell (only ten players used).

16/01/1897 v CHELTENHAM (A) Lost 0-2
A Cowley; JG Washbourne, WH Hicks; EHP Scantlebury, WT Pitt, WA Brown; AJ Stephens, WH Godby,
ET James, HW Arkell, H Daniells.

06/02/1897 v PRICE WALKERS (H) Lost 1-2
WH Godby; JG Washbourne, WH Hicks; EHP Scantlebury, WT Pitt, WA Brown; AJ Stephens, AF Fielding,
A Roberts, ET James, HW Arkell.
Scorer: Roberts.

13/02/1897 v CIRENCESTER (H) Lost 0-2
A Cowley; AP Frith, WH Hicks; JG Washbourne, AF Fielding, WA Brown; AJ Stephens, A Flower,
JC Hammond, EHP Scantlebury, HW Arkell.

20/02/1897 v DEAN CLOSE SCHOOL (A) ?
A Cowley; WH Hicks, JG Washbourne; AC Cragg, WT Pitt, WA Brown; AJ Stephens, EHP Scantlebury,
ET James, HW Arkell, AN Other.

27/02/1897 v ROSS TOWN (H) Lost 1-2
? Bradford; WH Hicks, JG Washbourne; EHP Scantlebury, WT Pitt, WA Brown; AJ Stephens, HW Arkell, AC
Cragg, ET James, H Daniells.
Scorer: Craggs.

27/03/1897 v WYCLIFFE COLLEGE (H) ?
A Cowley; WH Hicks, JG Washbourne; P Jew, ? Baldwin, WA Brown; W Badham, ET Talbot, AJ Stephens,
HW Arkell, W Bellows.

1 game missing.

A statistic in a future Citizen indicated that Gloucester had played 16 friendlies this season.

09/10/1897 v WOTTON-UNDER-EDGE (A) Drew 0-0
F Hallett (Only one player mentioned in The Dursley, Berkeley & Sharpness Gazette & Wotton-Under-Edge Advertiser)

16/10/1897 v BRIDSTOW (A) ?
G Speck; WH Hicks, JG Washbourne; WA Brown, F Luker, JA Oakey; HW Arkell, SS Harris, G Eardley, AJ Stephens, LA Lane.

23/10/1897 v GORDON WANDERERS (H) ?
G Speck; WH Hicks, JG Washbourne; WA Brown, F Luker, JA Oakey; HW Arkell, AF Fielding, SS Harris, AJ Stephens, LA Lane.

06/11/1897 v STROUD (H) Won 3-2
LA Lane, HT Porter (Only two mentioned in The Citizen)
Scorers: Lane (2), Porter.

11/12/1897 v DEAN CLOSE SCHOOL (A) Won 5-0
HW Arkell, AF Fielding, LA Lane, G Saunders (Only four mentioned in The Citizen)
Scorers: Arkell (3), Lane or Saunders, AF Fielding.

08/01/1898 v STROUD (A) Won 7-2
HW Arkell, HT Porter, AF Fielding, G Saunders (Only four mentioned in The Citizen)
Scorers: Arkell (2), Porter, AF Fielding (2), Saunders, ?. (1 goal missing).

19/02/1898 v DEAN CLOSE SCHOOL (H) Won 4-0
GJA Beard, G Saunders (Only two mentioned in The Citizen)
Scorers: Beard (2), Saunders, own goal.

12/03/1898 v CIRENCESTER RAC (H) Won 4-0
JA Oakey, A Collins, LA Lane (Only three mentioned in The Citizen)
Scorers: Oakey (2), Collins, Lane.

19/03/1898 v GORDON WANDERERS (A) Won 3-0
G Speck; WH Hicks, JG Washbourne; A Rodway, WA Brown, JA Oakey; HW Arkell, J Stocks, A Collins, GJA Beard, G Saunders.
Scorers: Collins, own goal, ?. (1 goal missing).

26/03/1898 v WOTTON-UNDER-EDGE (H) cancelled

01/10/1898 v DEAN CLOSE SCHOOL (A) Won 2-0
AF Fielding (Only this player mentioned in The Citizen)
Scorers: AF Fielding, ?. (1 goal missing).

19/11/1898 v WOTTON-UNDER-EDGE (H) Won 3-0
(The Citizen missing at the Record Office)
Scorers: ?. (3 goals missing).
Originally Mid Gloucestershire League, Wotton-under-Edge withdrew

26/11/1898 v WYCLIFFE COLLEGE (H) Won 4-0
(The Citizen missing at the Record Office)
Scorers: ?. (4 goals missing).

14/01/1899 v BRISTOL AMATEURS (A) Lost 0-5 (Gloucestershire County Cup 1st Round)
G Speck; AP Frith, HW Arkell; SS Harris, AF Fielding, JA Oakey; BH Lane, HT Porter, LA Lane, HG Sherwood, W Long.

04/02/1899 v DEAN CLOSE SCHOOL (H) abandoned

25/03/1899 v BRIMSCOMBE (A) Won 4-1
W Jones; SS Harris, HW Arkell; LA Lane, H Lane, RR Sly; AF Fielding, FT Rust, HG Sherwood, W Long, HT Porter.
Scorers: Long (2), AF Fielding, Rust.

30/09/1899 v DEAN CLOSE SCHOOL (A) Won 2-1
JW Stock, FT Rust, HT Porter (only three players mentioned in The Citizen)
Scorers: Stock, Porter.

21/10/1899 v TEWKESBURY ABBEY (A) Drew 1-1 (Gloucestershire FA Junior Cup)
F Hallett; E Keys, ? Langley-Smith; H Lane, ? Robotham, RR Sly; FT Rust, JW Stock, ? Carpenter, WJ Hart, W Merry.
Scorer: Carpenter.

04/11/1899 v SAINT MICHAEL'S (H) Lost 0-1
RR Sly, HT Porter (only two players mentioned in The Citizen)

11/11/1899 v TEWKESBURY ABBEY (H) Lost 0-1 (Gloucestershire FA Junior Cup Replay)
F Hallett; ? Langley-Smith, E Keys; ? Robotham, RR Sly, AN Other; FT Rust, JW Stock, WJ Hart, W Merry, AN Other.

27/01/1900 v STAPLE HILL (A) Lost (Gloucestershire Senior Cup)
RR Sly, HT Porter (only two players mentioned in The Citizen)

22/09/1900 v BERKELEY (A) Won 9-1
(No match report in The Citizen)
Scorers: ?. (9 goals missing).

06/10/1900 v TEWKESBURY ABBEY (A) Lost 2-3
(No match report in The Citizen)
Scorers: ?. (2 goals missing).

13/10/1900 v CHELTENHAM TOWN (A) Won 3-2
W Willetts; J Wakefield, W Shaw, W Mason, FT Rust (only five players mentioned in The Citizen)
Scorers: Wakefield, Rust.

20/10/1900 v WYCLIFFE COLLEGE (Mid Gloucestershire League)
Unplayed match. Wycliffe College had withdrawn from League.

MATCH SCHEDULED FOR 02/02/1901 POSTPONED DUE TO QUEEN VICTORIA'S DEATH

23/02/1901 v CHELTENHAM TOWN (H) (possibly a Cup match)
W Willetts; AF Fielding, HW Arkell; FR Crawley, DE Griffiths, T Axford; HT Porter, J Wakefield, W Shaw, C Wilson, FT Rust.
The re-arranged game I could not find in The Citizen. The match report(!) read thus: *'This match was down for decision at the Avenue Ground but only the Gloucester goal-keeper (Willetts) and our representative put in an appearance, and after waiting till 3:30 o'clock they left the field.'* The above team was selected for 23/02/1901.

02/03/1901 v BERKELEY (H) postponed
Recorded in The Citizen *'The return fixture, which was down for decision on the Avenue Ground, has been cried off owing to Berkeley being engaged in a Dursley & District League fixture.'*

20/09/1902 v STONEHOUSE (A) Won 2-1
W Willetts; EF Davy, WD Vinson; TH Rust, CFB Eddowes, FR Crawley; HT Porter, AG Gardner, FT Rust, AF Fielding, FCJ Romans.
Scorers: FT Rust (2).

04/10/1902 v BRIMSCOMBE (H) Won 5-1
W Willetts; HW Arkell, EF Davy; RR Sly, CFB Eddowes, FR Crawley; FCJ Romans, AF Fielding, FT Rust, A Parker, HT Porter.
Scorers: Parker, Eddowes, ? (3 goals missing).

11/10/1902 v TEWKESBURY ABBEY (A) Lost 1-2
W Willetts; EF Davy, HW Arkell; RR Sly, CFB Eddowes, FR Crawley; FCJ Romans, AF Fielding, FT Rust, A Parker, HT Porter.
Scorer: Rust.

18/10/1902 v WORCESTER NONDESCRIPTS (A) Won 7-3
W Willetts; EF Davy, HW Arkell; FR Crawley, CFB Eddowes, RR Sly; HT Porter, A Parker, AF Fielding, FCJ Romans (only ten players used. FT Rust missed the train).
Scorers: Romans (3), Parker (2), Fielding, Arkell.

25/10/1902 v WYCLIFFE COLLEGE (A) Won 4-1
W Willetts; EF Davey, FR Crawley; DE Griffiths, CFB Eddowes, RR Sly; HT Porter, A Parker, FT Rust, AF Fielding, FCJ Romans.
Scorers: ?. (4 goals missing).

08/11/1902 v TEWKESBURY ABBEY (H) Won 3-0
W Willetts; EF Davy, HW Arkell; FR Crawley, CFB Eddowes, RR Sly; J Wakefield, A Parker, FT Rust, AF Fielding, FCJ Romans.
Scorers: Fielding, Parker, Rust.

15/11/1902 v SAINT ANNE'S (A) Won 3-2 (Gloucestershire FA Junior Cup 3rd Round)
W Willetts; EF Davey, HW Arkell; FR Crawley, CFB Eddowes, RR Sly; J Wakefield, A Parker, FT Rust, AF Fielding, FCJ Romans.
Scorers: Romans (2), Rust.

29/11/1902 v CIRENCESTER TOWN (A) Won 4-1
(No match report in The Citizen)
Scorers: ?. (4 goals missing).

THE CITIZEN 1st to 10th DECEMBER MISSING AT THE RECORD OFFICE

13/12/1902 v BOURTON ROVERS (H) Drew 1-1 (Gloucestershire FA Junior Cup Semi-Final)
W Willetts; EF Davy, HW Arkell; FR Crawley, CFB Eddowes, RR Sly; J Wakefield, A Parker, FT Rust, AF Fielding, FCJ Romans.
Scorer: Rust.

20/12/1902 v BOURTON ROVERS (A) Won 1-0 (Gloucestershire FA Junior Cup Semi-Final Replay)
W Willetts; EF Davy, HW Arkell; FR Crawley, CFB Eddowes, RR Sly; J Wakefield, GW Fowler, FT Rust, AF Fielding, FCJ Romans.
Scorer: Rust (pen).

26/12/1902 v WARMLEY (A) Won 3-1 (Gloucestershire FA Junior Cup Final)
W Willetts; EF Davy, HW Arkell; FR Crawley, CFB Eddowes, RR Sly; J Wakefield, A Parker, FT Rust, AF Fielding, FCJ Romans.
Scorers: Romans (2), Parker.
(First time this cup left Bristol).

24/01/1903 v WORCESTER NONDESCRIPTS (H) Won 2-0
J Hawkins; A Parker, HW Arkell; FR Crawley, AF Fielding, RR Sly; J Wakefield, GW Fowler, FT Rust, A Ward, FCJ Romans.
Scorers: ?. (2 goals missing).

31/01/1903 v CIRENCESTER TOWN (H) Won 5-0
J Hawkins; A Parker, HW Arkell; FR Crawley, TH Rust, RR Sly; J Wakefield, GW Fowler, FT Rust, AF Fielding, FCJ Romans.
Scorers: ?. (5 goals missing).

14/02/1903 v BRIMSCOMBE (A) Drew 2-2
W Willetts; RR Sly, AF Fielding, A Parker, FT Rust (only five players mentioned in The Citizen).
Scorers: Rust, ?. (1 goal missing).

19/09/1903 v CHELTENHAM TOWN (A) Lost 0-2
CFB Eddowes, L Peckover, ? Newland, W Smith, TH Rust, ?, Fisher (only six players mentioned in The Citizen).

03/10/1903 v ROSS TOWN (A) Won 7-2
J Hawkins; CFB Eddowes, A Lamb; FR Crawley, L Peckover, TH Rust; J Wakefield, A Parker, FT Rust, HP Ellis, AF Fielding.
Scorers: FT Rust (5), Fielding, Parker.

10/10/1903 v ROSS TOWN (H) abandoned
J Hawkins; EF Davy, CFB Eddowes; FR Crawley, L Peckover, TH Rust; J Wakefield, HP Ellis, A Parker, FT Rust, AF Fielding.
Match abandoned owing to Ross being unable to field a team.

31/10/1903 v DURSLEY (A) Won 4-1
? Atkins; CFB Eddowes, FT Rust, AF Fielding, ? Gillard (only four players mentioned in The Citizen and ? Atkins in The Dursley, Berkeley & Sharpness Gazette & Wotton-Under-Edge Advertiser).
Scorers: Eddowes, FT Rust (3).

14/11/1903 v KINGSWOOD ROVERS (A) Lost 0-1 (Gloucestershire FA Junior Cup)
(No match report in The Citizen)

09/01/1904 v BRIMSCOMBE (A) crushing Win
(No match report in The Citizen)

30/01/1904 v DURSLEY (H) abandoned

26/03/1904 v BRIMSCOMBE (H) scratched

22/09/1906 v BOURTON ROVERS (A) Won 4-0 (Originally a Gloucester & District League match. Bourton withdrew from League.
W Willetts; FW Dee, FE Quixley; BG Harris, AH Smith, AV Boughton; FEA Crouch, H Smith, FT Rust, WD Niblett, W Smith.
Scorers: ?. (4 goals missing).

29/09/1906 v SAINT PAUL'S UNITED (A) Lost 1-2
W Willetts; FW Dee, FE Quixley; BG Harris, AH Smith, AV Boughton; FEA Crouch, CH Haddon, WD Niblett,
W Smith, JM Baldwin.
Scorer: W Smith.
(Originally a Cheltenham & District League match. There seemed to be some dispute surrounding this match
and it was replayed 06/04/1907).

20/10/1906 v SWINDON AMATEURS (H) Won 5-2
W Willetts; AS Keeping, FE Quixley; GA Vinson, AV Boughton, AH Smith; FEA Crouch, CH Haddon,
N Squier, WD Niblett, W Smith.
Scorers: Haddon (2), Squier (3).

27/10/1906 v CHEPSTOW SAINT MARY'S (A) Lost 1-2
W Willetts; FE Taylor, FE Quixley; GA Vinson, AV Boughton, AH Smith; FEA Crouch, CH Haddon,
WD Niblett, AE Kent, W Smith.
Scorer: ?. (1 goal missing).

10/11/1906 v DURSLEY (H) Won 8-1
W Willetts; FW Dee, FE Quixley; GA Vinson, AV Boughton, AH Smith; FEA Crouch, H Smith, N Squier,
CH Haddon, JM Baldwin.
Scorers: Squier (4), Haddon (2), Crouch (2).

17/11/1906 v CHELTENHAM TOWN (A) Won 4-2 (Gloucestershire FA Junior Cup)
W Willetts; EF Davy, FE Quixley; GA Vinson, AV Boughton, AH Smith; WD Niblett, H Smith, N Squier,
CH Haddon, JM Baldwin.
Scorers: Squier, H Smith, Baldwin, own goal.

01/12/1906 v KINGSWOOD ROVERS (A) Won 2-0 (Gloucestershire FA Junior Cup)
W Willetts; FE Taylor, FE Quixley; GA Vinson, AV Boughton, AH Smith; WD Niblett, CH Haddon, N Squier,
H Smith, JM Baldwin.
Scorers: Baldwin, Haddon.

22/12/1906 v SWINDON TOWN RESERVES (A) Lost 0-2
W Willetts; EF Davy, FE Quixley; GA Vinson, AV Boughton, AH Smith; OJA Carter, H Smith,
Wilfred Nicholls, W Smith, JM Baldwin.

26/12/1906 v WARMLEY AMATEURS (A) Lost 0-5 (Gloucester FA Junior Cup Final)
W Willetts; EF Davy, FE Quixley; GA Vinson, AV Boughton, AH Smith; CH Haddon, H Smith,
Wilfred Nicholls, W Smith, JM Baldwin.
(This line-up courtesy of Gloucester City AFC Diamond Jubilee Booklet, 1949).

12/01/1907 v BRIMSCOMBE (H) Won 2-1
W Willetts; EF Davy, FE Quixley; GA Vinson, AH Smith, AV Boughton; W Smith, CH Haddon,
Wilfred Nicholls, H Smith, Walter Nicholls.
Scorer: Wilfred Nicholls (2).

19/01/1907 v CHELTENHAM TRAINING COLLEGE (A) scratched

26/01/1907 v SWINDON TOWN RESERVES (H) Lost 4-5
W Willetts; EF Davy, FE Quixley; GA Vinson, AV Boughton, AH Smith; W Smith, H Smith, N Squier,
CH Haddon, JM Baldwin.
Scorers: Squier, H Smith (2), Haddon.

16/02/1907 v BOURTON ROVERS (H) Originally a Gloucester & District League match. Bourton withdrew.

16/03/1907 v SWINDON AMATEURS (A) Won 3-1
W Willetts; EF Davy, FE Quixley; GA Vinson, AH Smith; CH Haddon, AJ Carter, N Squier, C Barnes, W Smith (only ten players used. C Bain pulled out).
Scorers: ?. (3 goals missing).

30/03/1907 v BRIMSCOMBE (A) Drew 1-1
WD Vinson, AV Boughton, ? Cox (only these three players mentioned in The Citizen).
Scorer: Boughton.

13/04/1907 v REST OF CHELTENHAM & DISTRICT LEAGUE (A) Won 2-1
W Willetts; EF Davy, FE Quixley; GA Vinson, AV Boughton, AH Smith; CH Haddon, H Smith, AJ Carter, AE Kent, W Smith.
Scorers: Carter, Kent.

21/09/1907 v SWINDON TOWN RESERVES (A) Lost 0-3   Att: 3,000
WT Blake; EF Davy, WD Vinson; GA Vinson, AV Boughton, J Hill; OJ Lucas, H Smith, N Squier, AJ Carter, AE Kent.

05/10/1907 v SAINT PAUL'S TRAINING COLLEGE (A) Won 3-2
WT Blake; EF Davy, WD Vinson; GA Vinson, AV Boughton, AH Smith; OJ Lucas, R Turner, N Squier, AJ Carter, AE Kent.
Scorers: Squier, Turner, Lucas.

19/10/1907 v SWINDON TOWN RESERVES (H) Lost 0-1
WT Blake; EF Davy, WD Vinson; GA Vinson, AV Boughton, J Hill; OJ Lucas, R Turner, N Squier, AJ Carter, AE Kent.

09/11/1907 v BATH CITY (H) scratched

16/11/1907 v CLEVEDON (A) Lost 1-5 (English Amateur Cup Semi-Final Qualifying Round)
WT Blake; EF Davy, FE Quixley; GA Vinson, AV Boughton, AH Smith; OJ Lucas, R Turner, N Squier, AJ Carter, AE Kent.
Scorer: Kent.

07/12/1907 v BRISTOL CITY RESERVES (A) Lost 2-3
WC Vickery; EF Davy, FE Quixley; GA Vinson, AV Boughton, AH Smith; OJ Lucas, AJ Carter, N Squier, R Turner, AE Kent.
Scorers: Turner, Squier.

14/12/1907 v DURSLEY (A) Won 6-1
WC Vickery; EF Davy, FE Quixley; GA Vinson, AV Boughton, AH Smith; OJ Lucas, AJ Carter, N Squier, W Smith, AE Kent.
Scorers: Own goal, Squier (2), Lucas, Smith (2).
(Scorers courtesy of The Dursley, Berkeley & Sharpness Gazette & Wotton-Under-Edge Advertiser)

28/12/1907 v BRISTOL CITY RESERVES (H) Lost 1-5
WC Vickery; EF Davy, FE Quixley; GA Vinson, CFB Eddowes, AH Smith; OJ Lucas, AJ Carter, BG Harris, R Turner, W Smith.
Scorer: Harris.

18/01/1908 v CHELTENHAM TOWN (H) 1-0 (match abandoned after 25 minutes. Was a North Gloucestershire League game)
WC Vickery; EF Davy, FE Quixley; GA Vinson, AV Boughton, AH Smith; AE Kent, AJ Carter, N Squier, R Turner, F Bottomley.
Scorer: Turner.

01/02/1908 v WARMLEY AMATEURS (H) Drew 1-1 (Gloucestershire FA County Intermediate Cup 2nd Round)
WC Vickery; EF Davy, FE Quixley; GA Vinson, AV Boughton, AH Smith; AE Kent, AJ Carter, N Squier, CH Haddon, F Bottomley.
Scorer: ?. (1 goal missing).

08/02/1908 v WARMLEY AMATEURS (A) Lost 0-2 (Gloucestershire FA County Intermediate Cup 2nd Round Replay)
WC Vickery; EF Davy, RM Parker; GA Vinson, AV Boughton, AH Smith; CH Haddon, OJ Lucas, N Squier, AJ Carter, AE Kent.

04/04/1908 v CHELTENHAM TRAINING COLLEGE (H) Lost 1-4
GB Brace; EF Davy, FE Quixley; GA Vinson, AV Boughton, J Hill; AH Adams, AH Smith, OJ Lucas, AJ Carter, C Carter.
Scorer: Davey.

20/04/1908 v REST OF NORTH GLOUCESTERSHIRE LEAGUE (A, Sharpness) Drew 3-3
AJ Carter, BG Harris, AE Kent (only three players mentioned in The Citizen).
Scorers: Carter, Harris, Kent.

11/09/1908 v SWINDON TOWN RESERVES (A) Lost 1-7
WC Vickery; WD Vinson, FE Quixley; GA Vinson, AH Smith, J Hill; T Wall, CH Haddon, N Squier, AE Kent, W Smith.
Scorer: Squier.

18/09/1908 v BRIMSCOMBE (A) Drew 3-3
WC Vickery; WD Vinson, FE Quixley; GA Vinson, AH Smith, J Hill; E Simpson, N Squier, A Watts, AJ Carter, AE Kent.
Scorers: Squier, Watts (2).

25/09/1908 v COLWALL (H) Won 3-2
WC Vickery; FE Quixley, FE Taylor; AH Smith, AV Boughton, GA Vinson; E Simpson, A Watts, N Squier, AJ Carter, AE Kent.
Scorers: Squier (3).
***Note: Gloucester City appeared in new colours of black and white.

10/10/1908 v STROUD (A) Drew 2-2
WC Vickery; FE Taylor, FE Quixley; GA Vinson, AV Boughton, AH Smith; E Simpson, W Smith, A Watts, AJ Carter, AE Kent.
Scorers: Carter, Watts.

17/10/1908 v COLWALL (A) Lost 0-5
WC Vickery; RM Palmer, FE Quixley; GA Vinson, R Middlecote, CE Brown; AE Kent, A Watts, AJ Carter, JT Parsons, W Smith.

31/01/1908 v SAINT PAUL'S TRAINING COLLEGE (H) Lost 4-5
WC Vickery; RM Palmer, FE Quixley; GA Vinson, WA Jarman, AH Smith; AE Kent, A Watts, E Simpson, JT Parsons, W Smith.
Scorers: W Smith, Watts (2,1 pen), Parsons.

07/11/1908 v WANTAGE TOWN (H) Wantage scratched (English Amateur Cup 3rd Round)

28/11/1908 v HEREFORD CITY (A) Lost 2-4 (English Amateur Cup 4th Round)
WC Vickery; WD Vinson, FE Quixley; GA Vinson, AH Smith, J Hill; AE Kent, A Watts, N Squier, AJ Carter, W Smith.
Scorer: W Smith (2).

26/12/1908 v TEWKESBURY TOWN (A) Won 2-0
WC Vickery; EF Davey, FE Quixley; GA Vinson, S Fawkes, CE Brown; GB Brace, RM Palmer, BG Harris,
L Butler, W Smith.
Scorer: Harris (2).

09/01/1909 v SWINDON TOWN RESERVES (H) Lost 2-3
WC Vickery; WD Vinson, FE Quixley; GA Vinson, AH Smith, J Hill; S Cook, BG Harris, WA Jarman,
AJ Carter, W Smith.
Scorers: Jarman, Carter.

06/02/1909 v WARMLEY AMATEURS (A) Lost 0-2 (Gloucestershire FA Intermediate Cup 2nd Round)
WC Vickery; WD Vinson, FE Quixley; GA Vinson, AH Smith, J Hill; S Cook, A Watts, WA Jarman, W Smith,
AE Kent.

06/03/1909 v STROUD (H) snowed off
A Goodman; WD Vinson, FE Quixley; GA Vinson, AH Smith, J Hill; S Cook, A Watts, AE Kent, W Smith,
AN Other.

27/03/1909 v SAINT PAUL'S TRAINING COLLEGE (A) Result unknown
WC Vickery; WD Vinson, FE Quixley; GA Vinson, AH Smith, J Hill; E Simpson, S Cook, A Goodman,
A Watts, AE Kent.

10/04/1909 v TEWKESBURY TOWN (A) Drew 2-2
EF Davey, A Watts, E Simpson (only two players mentioned in The Citizen and E Simpson in The Tewkesbury
Register).
Scorers: Watts (pen), Davey.
(This match was for the benefit of R Wathen, a Tewkesbury Town Reserve who damaged his leg)

17/04/1909 v REST OF NORTH GLOUCESTERSHIRE LEAGUE (N, Sharpness) Lost 2-3
WC Vickery; WD Vinson, FE Quixley; GA Vinson, AH Smith (OJ Lucas), J Hill; S Cook, E Simpson,
WA Jarman, A Watts, AE Kent.
Scorers: Lucas, Carter.

23/10/1909 v STROUD (A) Won 5-2 (English Amateur Cup 2nd Round)
WC Vickery; A Watts, J Hill; S Cook, WA Jarman, W Smith, AE Kent (only seven players mentioned in The
Citizen).
Scorers: Jarman, Cook, Smith (2), own goal.

06/11/1909 v SWINDON AMATEURS (A) Drew 2-2 (English Amateur Cup 3rd Round)
WC Vickery; JG Eldridge, W Ingles; GA Vinson, A Watts, AH Smith; S Cook, N Squier, WA Jarman, W Smith,
AE Kent.
Scorers: Squier, Jarman.

13/11/1909 v SWINDON AMATEURS (H) Won 3-2 (English Amateur Cup 3rd Round Replay)
WC Vickery; W Ingles, AH Smith; GA Vinson, A Watts, J Hill; S Cook, N Squier, WA Jarman, W Smith,
AE Kent.
Scorers: Kent (2), Cook.

27/11/1909 v HEREFORD CITY (A) Lost 1-4 (English Amateur Cup 4th Round)
WC Vickery; W Ingles, AH Smith; GA Vinson, A Watts, J Hill; S Cook, L Bathurst, WA Jarman, W Smith,
AE Kent.
Scorer: Jarman.

04/12/1909 v WINCHCOMBE TOWN (A) abandoned after 5 minutes due to snowstorm (Cheltenham & District League)
WC Vickery; W Ingles, LA Carleton; GA Vinson, WA Jarman, J Hill; AE Kent, W Smith, N Squier, AN Other, L Bathurst.

01/01/1910 v WARMLEY ATHLETIC (H) Won 2-0 (Gloucestershire FA County Intermediate Cup 1st Round)
WC Vickery; FE Quixley, LA Carleton; GA Vinson, AH Smith, J Hill; C Carter, W Smith, WA Jarman, JT Parsons, W Ingles.
Scorer: Parsons (2).

05/02/1910 v BRISTOL AMATEURS (H) Lost 2-4 (Gloucestershire FA County Intermediate Cup 2nd Round)
WC Vickery; LA Carleton, W Ingles; GA Vinson, A Watts, CG Carter; S Cook, JT Parsons, WA Jarman, W Smith, AE Kent.
Scorers: Jarman, Parsons.

17/02/1910 v BRIMSCOMBE (H) postponed (North Gloucestershire League)
WC Vickery: LA Carleton, W Ingles; GA Vinson, A Watts, CG Carter; S Cook, AH Smith, WA Jarman, W Smith, AE Kent.
Ground a veritable quagmire.

17/03/1910 v SWINDON TOWN RESERVES (A) Lost 1-4
WC Vickery; LA Carleton, W Ingles; GA Vinson, AH Smith, CG Carter; S Cook, A Watts, WA Jarman, W Smith, AE Kent.
Scorer: Jarman.

02/04/1910 v SWINDON TOWN RESERVES (H) Lost 2-3
WC Vickery; ? Trueman, LA Carleton; GA Vinson, A Watts, J Hill; AE Kent, AH Smith, WA Jarman, W Smith, W Ingles.
Scorers: Kent, Jarman.

09/04/1910 v SAINT PAUL'S UNITED (H) abandoned, visitors never turned up (North Gloucestershire League)
WC Vickery; W Ingles, LA Carleton; GA Vinson, A Watts, CG Carter; S Cook, AH Smith, WA Jarman, W Smith, AE Kent.

1909/1910 v WINCHCOMBE TOWN (A)
missing

20/09/1913 v LECKHAMPTON (A) ?
HGH Davoll; JM McFarlane, CA Bretherton; P Bygrave, JB Shadgett, FL Mills; ER Danks, EJ Jones, E Searles, EE Allen, JT Parsons.

27/09/1913 v HARTPURY (A) ?
HGH Davoll; JM McFarlane, CA Bretherton; JB Lane, JB Shadgett, FL Mills; ER Danks, EE Allen, HE Searles, LF Dudbridge, JT Parsons.

11/10/1913 v WYCLIFFE COLLEGE (A) Lost 2-10
HGH Davoll; JM McFarlane, CA Bretherton; JB Lane, JB Shadgett, FL Mills; ER Danks, C Durrett, EJ Jones, EE Allen, JT Parsons.
Scorers: ?. (2 goals missing)

25/10/1913 v MARLING SCHOOL (A) ?
HGH Davoll; JM McFarlane, CA Bretherton; P Bygrave, JB Shadgett, JB Lane; ER Danks, LC Creber, EJ Jones, JT Parsons, P Horne.

22/11/1913 v SAINT CATHARINE'S Won 2-0
(Only this one player mentioned in The Citizen) ER Danks.
Scorer: Danks (2).

17/01/1914 v LECKHAMPTON (H) Drew 2-2
(Only two players mentioned in The Citizen) FL Mills, ER Danks.
Scorers: Danks, Mills.

31/01/1914 v SAINT GEORGE'S UNITED (A) Drew 2-2
(No information in The Citizen)

07/02/1914 v MITCHELDEAN (A) Lost 0-2 (Originally a North Gloucestershire League match. Deemed null and void)
HGH Davoll; JM McFarlane, CA Bretherton; JB Lane, JB Shadgett, FL Mills; ER Danks, EE Allen, EJ Jones, JT Parsons, LF Dudbridge.

14/02/1914 v WYCLIFFE COLLEGE (H) ?
HGH Davoll; JM McFarlane, CA Bretherton; JB Shadgett, C Sides, JB Lane; H Peacock, EE Allen, EJ Jones, HE Cropper, LF Dudbridge.

28/02/1914 v RYECROFT (A) Lost 0-2
(No information in The Citizen)

OTHER PLAYERS WHO REPRESENTED GLOUCESTER/GLOUCESTER YMCA/GLOUCESTER CITY IN CUP OR FRIENDLY GAMES DURING THIS PERIOD 1889-1914 (TOTAL = 122)

Note: Throughout this period cup games and friendly games were played. I thought it would be remiss of me not to give those players who did not appear in League matches a mention and they are as follows:

ADAMS, A.H (W)
1907/08

ATKINS, ? (GK)
1903/04

BADHAM, W.L (W)
1896/97

BAGLEY, R (W)
1891/92

BALDWIN, ? (CH)
1896/97

BATES, E (FB)
1891/92
1892/93

BATHURST, L (IF)
1909/10

BEARD, G.J.A (IF)
1897/98

BELLOWS, W (W)
1896/97

BENFIELD, W. H (WH)
1891/92
1892/93

BEVAN, A (FB)
1890/91

BLAKE, J.H (W)
1889/90

BOLLAND, Rev. Arthur Middleton (W)
b. Qu4 1867 Kirkstall, Leeds, Yorks. d. ?
1890/91
1891/92

BONNOR, G.R (WH)
1889/90

BRADFORD, ? (GK)
1896/97

BRAZIER, J (IF)
1891/92

BRERETON, Rev. Henry Lloyd (FB)
b. 13/01/1864 South Molton, Devon d. ?
1889/90

BUCHANAN, W.L (GK)
1890/91

CARPENTER, ? (CF)
1899/00

CASSWELL, T (GK)
1890/91

CHADBORN, Arthur E (FB)
b.1870 Gloucester d ?
1889/90
Note: Brother of Charles Chadborn and Harold Chadborn.

CHADBORN, Charles Nugent (CF)
b. Qu4 1872 Gloucester d ?
1889/90
Note: Brother of Arthur Chadborn and Harold Chadborn.

CHADBORN, Harold J (HB)
b. 1871 Gloucester d. ?
1889/90
Note: Brother of Arthur Chadborn and Charles Chadborn.

CLEMENSON, R (CF)
1890/91

COLLINS, A (IF)
1897/98

COOKE, A.B (GK)
1889/90

COOPER, W (FB)
1889/90

COWLEY, A (GK)
1896/97

COX, ? (F)
1906/07

CREBER, L.C (IF)
1913/14

CREESE, Percy Edward (W)
b. Qu2 1870 Tewkesbury, Glos. d. ?
1889/90

CROFTS, J.M (W)
1892/93

CROPPER, H.E (IF)
1913/14

DARKIN, ? (GK)
1892/93

DAVIES, G.P (WH)
1889/90
1890/91

DREWETT, O (FB)
1889/90

EARDLEY, G (CF)
1897/98

ELLIS, H.P (IF)
1903/04

ELY, William A.S (HB)
b. 1869 Gloucester d. ?
1889/90
1890/91

FAWKES, S (CH)
1908/09

FISHER, ?
1903/04

FLETCHER, F (WH)
1889/90
1890/91

FLOWER, A (FB)
1896/97

FOREST, A (CF)
1892/93

GARDNER, A. (FB)
b c1871 d. ?
1889/90
1890/91

GARDNER, A.G (IF)
1902/03

GODBY, W.H (WH)
1896/97
Note: Club Captain 1896-97.

GOODMAN, A (CF)
1908/09

GREAVES, L (FB)
1890/91

GREEN, F.H (FB)
1891/92

GRIMLEY, Horace F (WH)
b. 1871 Staffs. d. ?
1889/90

GRIMSHAW, F.W (GK)
1889/90

HAMMOND, J.C (IF)
1896/97

HARE, W (FB)
1889/90

HARRIS, W.A (W)
1896/97

HENDERSON, C.M (CF)
1889/90
1890/91
1891/92

HIGGINSON, S (FB)
1889/90
1890/91

HOCKIN, Henry Valentine (CF)
b. c1864 Kent d. ?
1889/90
1890/91

HORNE, P (W)
1913/14

HORNSBY, R.H (GK)
1892/93

JEW, Percy (HB)
1896/97

JONES, A (W)
1891/92

JONES, H.W (IF)
1892/93

KING, A.S (W)
1889/90
1891/92

KING, J (W)
1890/91
1891/92

LANGLEY-SMITH, ? (FB)
1899/00

LEWIS, M.B (W)
1890/91

LUCKMAN, M.R (W)
1896/97

LUKER, Frank (CH)
b. Qu2 1877 Gloucester d. ?
1897/98

MACFARLANE, A.B (WH)
1889/90
1890/91
1891/92

MATTHEWS, A.A (WH)
1891/92

McLINTON, S (IF)
1892/93

MERRY, W (W)
1899/00

MIDDLECOTE, R (CH)
1908/09

MITCHELL, C (WH)
1890/91
Club Record: London Casuals, Gloucester +.

MITCHELL, E.J.D (CH)
1890/91

MUNRO, W (WH)
1889/90

MURCH, R (GK)
1889/90
Club Record: Gloucester, Clifton +.

NEWLAND, ?
1903/04

NICHOLLS, Walter Turner (W)
b. Qu3 1886 Gloucester d. ?
1906/07
Note: Brother of Wilfred Nicholls.

OAKLEY, ? (IF)
1890/91

PALMER, C.E (CF)
1890/91

PEACOCK, H (W)
1913/14

PENFOLD, R.S (FB)
1892/93

PERKINS, G.B (IF)
1889/90
1890/91
1891/92

PHILLIPS, G.R (WH)
1890/91

PINK, A (FB)
1889/90

PLATT, E (GK)
1889/90

PLATT, F.J (FB)
1889/90

POOLE, A (WH)
1891/92

POOLE, Charles
Frederick (IF)
b. Qu1 1860 Cambridge,
Cambs. d. Jamaica
1889/90
1890/91
1891/92
Note: Club Captain 1889-
90. Brother of Percy
Poole.

POOLE, Percy Watson
(WH)
b. Qu3 1870 Cambridge,
Cambs. d. ?
1890/91
Note: Brother of Charles
Poole.

POWELL, Trevor
Barrett (W)
b. Qu1 1871 Ross,
Herefordshire d. ?
1889/90
1891/92
Note: Trevor Powell also
played rugby for
Gloucester RFC.

PRINCE, T (FB)
1890/91

ROBERTS, A (CF)
1896/97

ROBOTHAM, ? (CH)
1899/00

ROBSON, A.H (IF)
1896/97

RODWAY, A (WH)
1897/98

RODWELL, J (WH)
1890/91

SABIN, J (CF)
1896/97

SAMPSON, T.G (FB)
1891/92

SAUNDERS, Frank
Etheridge (HB)
b. 26/08/1864 Brighton,
Sussex d. ?
1890/91
Club Record: Cambridge
University, Swifts,
Corinthians, Gloucester, St
Thomas Hospital +.
International Record:
England (1).

SCANTLEBURY,
Edward Hugh P (WH)
b. Qu4 1875 Aylesbury,
Bucks. d. ?
1896/97

SEWELL, Cyril Otto
Hudson (IF)
b. 19/12/1874
Pietermaritzburg, South
Africa d. 19/08/1951
Bexhill, Sussex
1895/96
Note: Played cricket for
Gloucestershire CCC
1895-1919 (Captain 1913-
14).

SPECK, John (GK)
b. Qu1 1866 Gloucester d.
?
1890/91
1891/92
1895/96
Club Record: Nelson
Villa, Gloucester, Price
Walkers +
Note: Brother of George
Speck and Walter Speck.

SPECK, Walter (IF)
b. Qu4 1869 Gloucester d.
?
1889/90
Note: Brother of George
Speck and John Speck.

TALBOT, E.T (CF)
1896/97

TAYLOR, ? (CH)
1894/95

TAYNTON, A.G (CH)
1889/90

TURNER, J.E (W)
1894/95

VICKERY, W.H (HB)
1889/90

VIGNE, P.A (FB)
1892/93
1893/94

WADE, Rev. Reginald D (W)
b. 1865 Marylebone, London d. ?
1889/90
1890/91
1892/93

WALKER, F (WH)
1891/92

WALL, T (W)
1908/09
Club Record: Cheltenham Training College, Gloucester City +.

WALTERS, ? (WH)
1890/91

WARD, G.J (WH)
1889/90

WHEATON, N.F (CH)
1889/90

WOOD, S (W)
1892/93

WOODWARD, G.H (WH)
1891/92
1892/93

WRIGHT, A (IF)
1891/92

WRIGHT, E.C (CF)
1895/96

DURING THIS PERIOD GLOUCESTER/GLOUCESTER CITY DID RUN A RESERVE TEAM ALSO IN LEAGUE FOOTBALL. JUST FOR THE RECORD I HAVE ADDED THE LEAGUE TABLES.

1894-1895 – MID GLOUCESTERSHIRE LEAGUE

POS	CLUB	P	W	D	L	F	A	PTS
1	GLOUCESTER RESERVES	12	10	1	1			21
2	WOTTON	12	8	2	2			18
3	CHALFORD	12	5	2	5			12
4	FOREST GREEN ROVERS	12	4	4	4			12
5	BRIMSCOMBE	12	4	3	5			11
6	STROUD	12	4	1	7			9
7	WICKWAR	12	1	1	10			3
		84	36	14	34			86

The table does not balance.

The names of the players with the cup – WT Pitt, A Spence, E Goodwin, E Clark, H Green, A Clutterbuck, HT Robins, L Hartland, H Benfield, WH Godby, J Radford, AP Frith.

1895-1896 – MID GLOUCESTERSHIRE LEAGUE

POS	CLUB	P	W	D	L	F	A	PTS
1	WOTTON	10	9	0	1	48	8	18
2	CHALFORD	10	7	1	2	19	12	15
3	STROUD +	9	5	0	4	19	18	11
4	DURSLEY SAINT JAMES *	9	1	2	6	13	28	6
5	NAILSWORTH +	8	1	2	5	9	18	5
6	GLOUCESTER RESERVES +	8	0	3	5	9	33	5
		54	23	8	23	117	117	60

+ Nailsworth v Gloucester Reserves and Stroud v Gloucester Reserves not played due to smallpox scare, one point each.
Dursley Saint James v Nailsworth, two points to Dursley Saint James as Nailsworth unable to raise team.

1899-1900 – GLOUCESTER AND DISTRICT LEAGUE – SECOND DIVISION

POS	CLUB	P	W	D	L	F	A	PTS
1	ROSELEIGH	14	11	1	2	40	16	23
2	CHARLTON RANGERS	14	10	1	3	30	13	21
3	SAINT MICHAEL'S	14	7	3	4	28	13	17
4	TEWKESBURY ABBEY RESERVES	14	6	3	5	30	19	15
5	GLOUCESTER RESERVES *	14	6	5	3	20	18	15
6	CHELTENHAM RESERVES	14	4	2	8	26	31	10
7	ATLAS	14	1	2	11	9	33	4
8	YMCA *	14	1	3	10	12	52	3
		112	46	20	46	195	195	108

* Two points deducted for ineligible player.

1900-1901 – GLOUCESTER AND DISTRICT LEAGUE – SECOND DIVISION

POS	CLUB	P	W	D	L	F	A	PTS
1	CHARLTON RANGERS =	12	11	0	1	36	11	22
2	TEWKESBURY ABBEY RESERVES +	12	7	2	3	27	16	16
3	SAINT MICHAEL'S +=	12	6	0	6	27	15	12
4	GLOUCESTER PIONEER	12	5	2	5	24	25	12
5	ROSELEIGH RESERVES *	12	5	1	6	23	20	9
6	GLOUCESTER RESERVES	12	3	1	8	11	30	7
7	CHELTENHAM RESERVES #	12	2	0	10	9	37	4
		84	39	6	39	157	154	82

* Roseleigh Reserves were penalised two points for playing three ineligible players against Saint Michael's and the match was ordered to be replayed.
+ Awarded two points each by reason of Cheltenham Reserves failing to keep their fixture. The matches have been reckoned as played.
= Awarded two points by reason of Gloucester Reserves failing to keep their fixture. The matches have been reckoned as played.

Awarded two points by reason of Roseleigh Reserves failing to keep their fixture. The matches have been reckoned as played.

1902-1903 – GLOUCESTER AND DISTRICT LEAGUE – SECOND DIVISION

POS	CLUB	P	W	D	L	F	A	PTS
1	SAINT MICHAEL'S	8	7	0	1	30	9	14
2	GLOUCESTER CITY RESERVES	8	4	0	4	17	13	8
3	TEWKESBURY UNITED	8	3	1	4	11	11	7
4	TEWKESBURY ABBEY RESERVES	8	3	1	4	6	21	7
5	CHELTENHAM RESERVES	8	1	2	5	13	23	4
		40	18	4	18	77	77	40

1903-1904 – GLOUCESTER AND DISTRICT LEAGUE – SECOND DIVISION

POS	CLUB	P	W	D	L	F	A	PTS
1	SAINT LUKE'S	9	7	1	1	30	8	15
2	GLOUCESTER CITY RESERVES *	9	5	1	3	17	8	13
3	SAINT MICHAEL'S RESERVES	9	5	2	2	29	10	12
4	CHARLTON ROVERS	7	4	0	3	11	11	8
5	TEWKESBURY RESERVES	8	2	0	6	11	15	4
6	HUCCLECOTE *	8	0	0	8	3	49	2
		50	23	4	23	100	101	54

* Tewkesbury Reserves did not fulfil fixtures so two points given to clubs indicated.
The Citizen of 26 March 1904 would indicate this as possible Final Table as winners of cups and medals announced.

1906-1907 – GLOUCESTER AND DISTRICT LEAGUE – SECOND DIVISION

POS	CLUB	P	W	D	L	F	A	PTS
1	LINDEN OLD BOYS	8	7	1	0	16	5	15
2	GLOUCESTER CITY RESERVES	6	2	2	2	14	6	6
3	NEWENT	4	0	1	3	2	11	1
4	TEWKESBURY RESERVES *	5	1	1	3	3	6	1
5	MATSON *	5	1	1	3	2	8	1
		28	11	6	11	37	36	24

* Two points deducted for ineligible player.
Fixtures incomplete.

1907-1908 – NORTH GLOUCESTERSHIRE LEAGUE – SECOND DIVISION

POS	CLUB	P	W	D	L	F	A	PTS
1	GLOUCESTER CITY RESERVES	8	6	1	1	33	6	13
2	TEWKESBURY RESERVES	8	5	1	2	27	12	11
3	NEWENT	8	5	0	3	18	11	10
4	BARNWOOD *	8	2	0	6	9	35	0
5	MIDLAND & SOUTH WESTERN JUNCTION RAILWAY RESERVES +	8	1	0	7	7	28	0
		40	19	2	19	94	92	34

* Lose four points playing ineligible men in two fixtures and goal scored in matches in question disallowed.
+ Lose two points playing ineligible man and goal scored in matches in question disallowed.

1908-1909 – NORTH GLOUCESTERSHIRE LEAGUE – SECOND DIVISION

POS	CLUB	P	W	D	L	F	A	PTS
1	GLOUCESTER CITY RESERVES	8	6	2	0	21	4	14
2	GLEVUM	7	4	2	1	18	4	10
3	NEWENT	8	3	1	4	15	15	7
4	TUFFLEY & WHADDON	6	2	1	3	5	8	5
5	TEWKESBURY RESERVES	8	0	2	6	9	36	2
		37	15	8	14	68	67	38

To early April 1909 only. No table printed at end of season.

1909-1910 – NORTH GLOUCESTERSHIRE LEAGUE – SECOND DIVISION

POS	CLUB	P	W	D	L	F	A	PTS
1	GLEVUM	8	7	1	0	34	10	15
2	NEWENT	7	1	5	1	11	9	6
3	GLOUCESTER CITY RESERVES *	7	2	2	3	12	7	4
4	STROUD RESERVES *	8	2	2	4	9	22	4
5	LONGHOPE	8	1	2	5	9	28	4
		38	13	12	13	75	76	33

* Two points deducted for playing ineligible player.
One match missing.

CLEAN UP OUR GAME

The message is simple: For the good of the game, end the excesses that are causing us all to shy away with embarrassment.

- End the foul and abusive language by fans, players and managers.
- Stop abuse of referees - both verbal and physical.
- Call time on player dissent.
- Kick out the divers and cheats feigning injury.

In short, give us back the game we knew and loved.

No one is suggesting that Non-League football is a hotbed of these problems. But we believe an example set by players and fans who are in the game for the love of the challenge rather than the lure of the cheque book will resonate around the country.

From small acorns grow giant oaks. From an idea begun in Non-League, so might the whole of football benefit.

NOTES